PUFFIN BOOKS

The First Young Puffi

Barbara Ireson was born in Eastbourne. Her hobbies include restoring old houses, collecting antiques and exploring France. Barbara is one of the best regarded anthologists for children. Her first collections were made over thirty years ago and are still in print. She has since compiled many successful and popular children's verse and story collections, several of which are in Puffin.

She is married to Clifford Ireson, Emeritus Professor of Modern French Literature. They now live in Vouvray, France, where Barbara is pursuing her writing as well as helping her two sons with their antiques business.

Other collections by Barbara Ireson

The Second Young Puffin Book of Bedtime Stories
The Third Young Puffin Book of Bedtime Stories
The Fourth Young Puffin Book of Bedtime Stories

Verse

The Young Puffin Book of Verse

For older readers

Fighting in Break and Other Stories
Haunting Tales
In a Class of Their Own

The First Young Puffin Book of Bedtime Stories

Chosen by Barbara Ireson

Illustrated by Glenys Ambrus and Caroline Sharpe

PUFFIN BOOKS

PUFFIN BOOKS

Published by the Penguin Group
Penguin Books Ltd, 27 Wrights Lane, London W8 5TZ, England
Penguin Books USA Inc., 375 Hudson Street, New York, New York 10014, USA
Penguin Books Australia Ltd, Ringwood, Victoria, Australia
Penguin Books Canada Ltd, 10 Alcorn Avenue, Toronto, Ontario, Canada M4V 3B2
Penguin Books (NZ) Ltd, 182–190 Wairau Road, Auckland 10, New Zealand

Penguin Books Ltd, Registered Offices: Harmondsworth, Middlesex, England

The stories in this collection were first published in *Story Chest: 100 Bedtime Stories* by Viking Kestrel 1986
Published in *Never Meddle with Magic* in Puffin Books 1988
This collection published in Puffin Books 1994
10 9 8 7 6 5 4 3 2

Filmset in Photina

Made and printed in England by Clays Ltd, St Ives plc

Contents

The Kidnapping of Clarissa Montgomery

'You'll only have to stay here till your rich guardian pays the ransom,' said the kidnapper, whose name was Humphrey. He felt rather sorry for poor little Clarissa. She hadn't said anything since they'd grabbed her from the luxurious grounds of her mansion that afternoon. 'I think the poor little kid's in shock,' Humphrey said worriedly to Spud, who had masterminded the abduction. Spud didn't care if she was in shock, neither did Milligan.

'Just sit tight and don't cause any trouble, kid,' Spud snarled; 'Soon as the old man pays the fifty thousand, you'll be sent back.'

Clarissa finally spoke. 'Fifty thousand?' she said.

'I'm sure he'll manage to find it,' said kind-hearted Humphrey reassuringly. 'You'll be out of here in no time.'

Clarissa looked at him coldly. 'You're all mad,' she said. 'You could have got a whole lot more than fifty thousand. My guardian is loaded.'

'She's in shock,' Humphrey thought, and made her a cup of cocoa with his own hands. He'd fixed up a corner of the barn quite nicely with a toffee apple in a saucer. He was fond of little kids.

Spud was setting up a poker game. Clarissa watched silently.

'You don't have to be scared of those gorillas,' Humphrey whispered. 'They're really harmless.'

'I'm not scared of anything,' Clarissa said, and drew closer to the table..

'Beat it,' growled Spud, but Clarissa looked at his card, then went round the table and inspected Humphrey's and Milligan's. 'Get rid of the red queen and keep the clubs,' she said to Humphrey, and he did, and won.

'Scat, kid,' said Spud, but Clarissa sat down at the table.

'I want to play, too,' she said.

'Go back to your cocoa,' Spud ordered, but Clarissa opened her mouth and let out a high-pitched wailing yell. It went on and on, unbearable in the galvanized-iron roofed barn, and Spud, Milligan and Humphrey covered their ears.

'Maybe she'll stop if we let her play,' suggested Humphrey, and dealt out a hand to Clarissa. She stopped screeching and picked up her cards. Then she proceeded, without any trouble at all, to win ten games and fifty dollars.

'It's not very nice, if you ask me,' Spud said disgustedly. 'Little girls shouldn't know how to cheat at poker.'

Clarissa pocketed her winnings and went to bed. She slept very well. In the morning she woke up early. Humphrey, Spud and Milligan were dozing fitfully in uncomfortable chairs. Clarissa made herself a substantial breakfast, then examined the barn.

'Get away from that door!' Spud said, waking up.

'I've seen play forts in council parks better defended than this old barn,' Clarissa scoffed. 'The police could have this place surrounded and you wouldn't even know. No wonder you only asked for fifty thousand. It's all you're worth.'

Spud was so indignant that he bit his pre-breakfast cigar in two. 'What became of all the food?' he demanded angrily.

'I had it for my breakfast, of course,' Clarissa said.

So Humphrey, Spud and Milligan had to make do with discussing the plans for collecting the ransom money instead. Clarissa listened. 'It won't work,' she jeered. 'Just how do you expect Humphrey to reach the hollow tree in the park past a whole lot of detectives all lying in wait? It's too corny, collecting ransom money from a hollow tree.'

'And what would you suggest then, Miss Smarty?' Spud asked.

'Some place where they can't set up an ambush, of course. Tell them to put the money in a briefcase in a plastic bag and drop it off the pier. One of you could get in wearing scuba gear. It's a much better plan than your old hollow tree. I'll draft a new anonymous letter to my rich guardian.' Clarissa began cutting letters from Spud's newspaper, even though he hadn't read the racing page yet. She pasted the letters to a sheet of paper, and even Spud had to admit that it looked much more professional than theirs. And she'd doubled the ransom money, too.

'But none of us can scuba dive,' Humphrey pointed out.

'I can,' said Clarissa crushingly. 'I'll collect the money. But only if you give me a share.'

'That's only right,' said Humphrey. 'If she picks it up, she should be given something.'

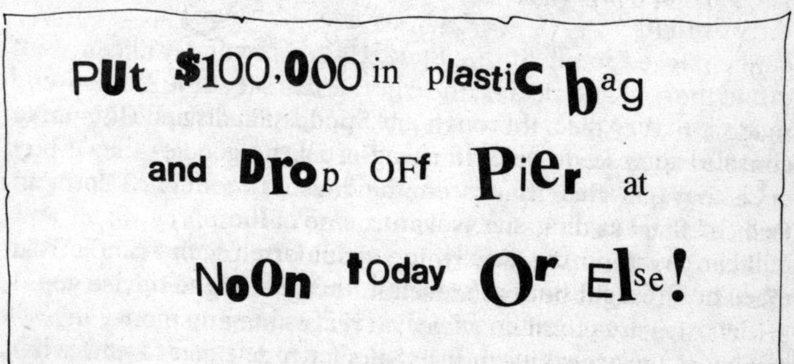

'Ninety-five per cent,' said Clarissa. 'Or I won't go at all. Anyhow, you wouldn't have any ransom money in the first place, if it wasn't for me.'

'If it wasn't for you, we wouldn't be sitting in this draughty old barn with nothing to eat for breakfast but a toffee apple,' said Spud. 'I wish we'd concentrated on stealing your rich guardian's valuable oil paintings instead.'

'You'd never get near them. They're fitted with electronic alarms.'

'I stole the Mona Lisa once,' Spud said boastfully.

'And you only got as far as the front door before they caught you. I read about it in the papers. The only way you could steal my guardian's paintings is if I came along and showed you the secret panel where you can cut off the alarm circuit. So there.'

Spud sourly began a round of poker while Humphrey went out to deliver the ransom note. Clarissa won another ten games. Spud thought with pleasure that after tonight they'd be rid of her. 'Soon as we pick up that briefcase, we'll drop you off at your mansion,' he said.

'First we'll come back here and count the money,' contradicted Clarissa. 'Don't you know you can't trust anyone? You're the most hopeless gang leader I ever met. And you'll have to make plans about leaving the country, too. You'll need to learn a foreign language, but that's no problem. This afternoon you can all study French verbs. I'll supervise. That's after you clean up the getaway car. I'm not going anywhere to pick up ransom money in a car as dirty as that.'

She nagged so much that Spud, Humphrey and Milligan went out in the cold and cleaned the car. Clarissa sat at the window and made sure they did a thorough job. Spud, Milligan and Humphrey consoled themselves with thinking of all the goodies they'd buy once they got their hands on the ransom money. 'A farm in France,' Spud said. 'I always wanted one of those.'

'I bet you don't know anything about farming, or France,' said Clarissa. 'It might be a good idea if I came along to advise you. I always give my guardian advice on real estate and money investment and I practically run his affairs for him. I don't know what he'd do without me.'

Milligan, Spud and even Humphrey eyed her with distaste. They were getting fed up with the draughty barn, the waiting and the French verbs, and most of all they were fed up with Clarissa and her organizing.

It was almost a relief when the time came to collect the ransom money. They drove to the waterfront, and Clarissa put on the scuba suit and galloped confidently into the sea.

'She might swim to the pier and just pop up and give the alarm,' said Humphrey nervously. 'Let's get out of here.'

'Not without our share of the money,' said Spud. 'I haven't put up with that kid all day for nothing.'

'We won't have to put up with her much longer,' said Milligan thankfully. 'Soon as we sort out the ransom money, we can drop her off at her mansion, and good riddance. Then it's off to the south of France for us.'

'That guardian's welcome to her,' said Spud. 'We should give the poor old fellow a few thousand dollars back. I feel sorry for him, having to put up with her till she's grown up and married.'

'No one would marry her,' said Milligan with conviction. 'Not even if they were bribed with all of the Montgomery fortune.'

They watched the water anxiously, but no police boat bristling with armed constables skimmed into sight. And after fifteen minutes Clarissa emerged, carrying a weighted briefcase in a plastic bag. Milligan, Spud and Humphrey tried to grab it from her, but Clarissa put it in the getaway car and sat on it. 'Don't be so greedy,' she said. 'You're making as much noise as kids in a sandpit. You'll just have to wait till we get back to the barn.'

On the way back the three gangsters were quite civil to Clarissa. They were all thinking that very soon they could drop her off at her mansion and never have to listen to her again or be ordered about.

Spud had the first try at the locked briefcase, and failed. Milligan failed, too, and then Humphrey had a turn, with his skilful hands that had foiled every bank safe in town. But even he couldn't get the combination lock open.

'What a lot of butterfingers!' said Clarissa, and turned the little numbered cylinder and the lid flew open.

But the briefcase wasn't full of bank notes at all. There wasn't anything but the bricks that had served to weigh it down in the water. And one short typed note. Spud snatched it up and read it aloud, and his eyes rounded with horror and disbelief.

DO NOT WANT CLARISSA BACK,
SHE IS TOO IRRITATING.
AND BOSSY. YOU CAN KEEP HER.
GLAD TO GET RID OF HER,
REGARDS, ALGERNON MONTGOMERY,
MILLIONAIRE.

All the kidnappers turned pale and sat down.

'Why are you all sitting down wasting time?' Clarissa demanded, frowning. 'We have an oil painting job to plan. And now that I'm in charge of this gang, I expect much better work from all of you.'

ROBIN KLEIN

In the Middle of the Night

In the middle of the night a fly woke Charlie. At first he lay listening, half-asleep, while it swooped about the room. Sometimes it was far; sometimes it was near – that was what had woken him; and occasionally it was very near indeed. It was very, very near when the buzzing stopped: the fly had alighted on his face. He jerked his head up; the fly buzzed off. Now he was really awake.

The fly buzzed widely about the room, but it was thinking of Charlie all the time. It swooped nearer and nearer. Nearer . . .

Charlie pulled his head down under the bedclothes. All of him under the bedclothes, he was completely protected; but he could hear nothing except his heartbeats and his breathing. He was overwhelmed by the smell of warm bedding, warm pyjamas, warm himself. He was going to suffocate. So he rose suddenly up out of the bedclothes; and the fly was waiting for him. It dashed at him. He beat at it with his hands. At the same time he appealed to his younger brother, Wilson, in the next bed: 'Wilson, there's a fly!'

Wilson, unstirring, slept on.

Now Charlie and the fly were pitting their wits against each other: Charlie pouncing on the air where he thought the fly must be; the fly sliding under his guard towards his face. Again and again the fly reached Charlie; again and again, almost simultaneously, Charlie dislodged him. Once he hit the fly – or, at least, hit where the fly had been a second before, on the side of his head; the blow was so hard that his head sang with it afterwards.

Then suddenly the fight was over; no more buzzing. His blows – or rather, one of them – must have told.

He laid his head back on the pillow, thinking of going to sleep again. But he was also thinking of the fly, and now he noticed a tickling in the ear he turned to the pillow.

It must be – it *was* – the fly.

He rose in such panic that the waking of Wilson really seemed to him a possible thing, and useful. He shook him repeatedly: 'Wilson – Wilson, I tell you, there's a fly in my ear!'

Wilson groaned, turned over very slowly like a seal in water, and slept on.

The tickling in Charlie's ear continued. He could just imagine the fly struggling in some passageway too narrow for its wingspan. He longed to put his finger into his ear and rattle it round, like a stick in a rabbit-hole, but he was afraid of driving the fly deeper into his ear.

Wilson slept on.

Charlie stood in the middle of the bedroom floor, quivering and trying to think. He needed to see down his ear, or to get someone else to see down it. Wilson wouldn't do; perhaps Margaret would.

Margaret's room was next door. Charlie turned on the light as he entered: Margaret's bed was empty. He was startled, and then thought that she must have gone to the lavatory. But there was no light from there. He listened carefully: there was no sound from anywhere, except for the usual snuffling moans from the hall, where Floss slept and dreamt of dog-biscuits. The empty bed was mystifying; but Charlie had his ear to worry about. It sounded as if there were a pigeon inside it now.

Wilson asleep; Margaret vanished; that left Alison. But Alison was bossy, just because she was the eldest; and, anyway, she would probably only wake Mum. He might as well wake Mum himself.

Down the passage and through the door always left ajar. 'Mum,' he said. She woke, or at least half-woke, at once: 'Who is it? Who? Who? What's the matter? What? –'

'I've a fly in my ear.'

'You can't have.'

'It flew in.'

She switched on the bedside light, and, as she did so, Dad plunged beneath the bedclothes with an exclamation and lay still again.

Charlie knelt at his mother's side of the bed and she looked into his ear. 'There's nothing.'

'Something crackles.'

'It's wax in your ear.'

'It tickles.'

'There's no fly there. Go back to bed and stop imagining things.'

His father's arm came up from below the bedclothes. The hand waved about, settled on the bedside light and clicked it out. There was an upheaval of bedclothes and a comfortable grunt.

'Good night,' said Mum from the darkness. She was already allowing herself to sink back into sleep again.

'Good night,' Charlie said sadly. Then an idea occurred to him. He repeated his good night loudly and added some coughing, to cover the fact that he was closing the bedroom door behind him – the door that Mum kept open so that she could listen for her children. They had outgrown all that kind of attention, except possibly for Wilson. Charlie had shut the door against Mum's hearing because he intended to slip downstairs for a drink of water – well, for a drink and perhaps a snack. That fly-business had woken him up and also weakened him: he needed something.

He crept downstairs, trusting to Floss's good sense not to make a row. He turned the foot of the staircase towards the kitchen, and there had not been the faintest whimper from her, far less a bark. He was passing the dog-basket when he had the most unnerving sensation of something being wrong there – something unusual, at least. He could not have said whether he had heard something or smelt something – he could certainly have seen nothing in the blackness: perhaps some extra sense warned him.

'Floss?' he whispered, and there was the usual little scrabble and snuffle. He held out his fingers low down for Floss to lick. As she did not do so at once, he moved them towards her, met some obstruction –

'Don't poke your fingers in my eyes!' a voice said, very low-toned and cross. Charlie's first, confused thought was that Floss had spoken: the voice was familiar – but then a voice from Floss should *not* be familiar; it should be strangely new to him –

He took an uncertain little step towards the voice, tripped over the obstruction, which was quite wrong in shape and size to be Floss, and sat down. Two things now happened. Floss, apparently having climbed over the obstruction, reached his lap and began to lick his face. At the same time a human hand fumbled over his face, among the slappings of Floss's tongue, and settled over his mouth. 'Don't make a row! Keep quiet!' said the same voice. Charlie's mind cleared: he knew, although without understanding, that he was sitting on the floor in the dark with Floss on his knee and Margaret beside him.

Her hand came off his mouth.

'What are you doing here, anyway, Charlie?'

'I like that! What about you? There was a fly in my ear.'

'Go on!'

'There was.'

'Why does that make you come downstairs?'

'I wanted a drink of water.'

'There's water in the bathroom.'

'Well, I'm a bit hungry.'

'If Mum catches you . . .'

'Look here,' Charlie said, 'you tell me what you're doing down here.'

Margaret sighed. 'Just sitting with Floss.'

'You can't come down and just sit with Floss in the middle of the night.'

'Yes, I can. I keep her company. Only at weekends, of course. No one seemed to realize what it was like for her when those puppies went. She just couldn't get to sleep for loneliness.'

'But the last puppy went weeks ago. You haven't been keeping Floss company every Saturday night since then.'

'Why not?'

Charlie gave up. 'I'm going to get my food and drink,' he said. He went into the kitchen, followed by Margaret, followed by Floss.

They all had a quick drink of water. Then Charlie and Margaret looked into the larder: the remains of a joint; a very large quantity of mashed potato; most of a loaf; eggs; butter; cheese . . .

'I suppose it'll have to be just bread and butter and a bit of cheese,' said Charlie. 'Else Mum might notice.'

'Something hot,' said Margaret. 'I'm cold from sitting in the hall comforting Floss. I need hot cocoa, I think.' 'She poured some milk into a saucepan and put it on the hot plate. Then she began a search for the tin of cocoa. Charlie, standing by the cooker, was already absorbed in the making of a rough cheese sandwich.

The milk in the pan began to steam. Given time, it rose in the saucepan, peered over the top, and boiled over on to the hot plate, where it sizzled loudly. Margaret rushed back and pulled the saucepan to one side. 'Well, really, Charlie! Now there's that awful smell! It'll still be here in the morning, too.'

'Set the fan going,' Charlie suggested.

The fan drew the smell from the cooker up and away through a pipe to the outside. It also made a loud roaring noise. Not loud enough to reach their parents, who slept on the other side of the house – that was all that Charlie and Margaret thought of.

Alison's bedroom, however, was immediately above the kitchen. Charlie was eating his bread and cheese, Margaret was drinking her cocoa, when the kitchen door opened and there stood Alison. Only Floss was pleased to see her.

'Well!' she said.

Charlie muttered something about a fly in his ear, but Margaret said nothing. Alison had caught them red-handed. She would call Mum downstairs, that was obvious. There would be an awful row.

Alison stood there. She liked commanding a situation.

Then, instead of taking a step backwards to call up the stairs to Mum, she took a step forward into the kitchen. 'What are you having, anyway?' she asked. She glanced with scorn at Charlie's poor piece of bread and cheese and at Margaret's cocoa. She moved over to the larder, flung open the door, and looked searchingly inside. In such a way must Napoleon have viewed a battlefield before victory.

Her gaze fell upon the bowl of mashed potato. 'I shall make potato-cakes,' said Alison.

They watched while she brought the mashed potato to the kitchen table. She switched on the oven, fetched her other ingredients, and began mixing.

'Mum'll notice if you take much of that potato,' said Margaret.

But Alison thought big. 'She may notice if some potato is missing,' she agreed. 'But if there's none at all, and if the bowl it was in is washed and dried and stacked away with the others, then she's going to think she must have made a mistake. There just can never have been any mashed potato.'

Alison rolled out her mixture and cut it into cakes; then she set the cakes on a baking-tin and put it in the oven.

Now she did the washing up. Throughout the time they were in the kitchen, Alison washed up and put away as she went along. She wanted no one's help. She was very methodical, and she did everything herself to be sure that nothing was left undone. In the morning there must be no trace left of the cooking in the middle of the night.

'And now,' said Alison, 'I think we should fetch Wilson.'

The other two were aghast at the idea; but Alison was firm in her reasons. 'It's better if we're all in this together, Wilson as well. Then if the worst comes to the worst, it won't be just us three caught out, with Wilson hanging on to Mum's apron-strings, smiling innocence. We'll all be for it together; and Mum'll be softer with us if we've got Wilson.'

They saw that at once. But Margaret still objected: 'Wilson will tell. He just always tells everything. He can't help it.'

Alison said, 'He always tells everything. Right: we'll give him something *to* tell, and then see if Mum believes him. We'll do an entertainment for him. Get an umbrella from the hall and Wilson's sou'wester and a blanket or a rug or something. Go on.'

They would not obey Alison's orders until they had heard her plan; then they did. They fetched the umbrella and the hat, and lastly they fetched Wilson, still sound asleep, slung between them in his eiderdown. They propped him in a chair at the kitchen table, where he still slept.

By now the potato-cakes were done. Alison took them out of the oven and set them on the table before Wilson. She buttered them, handing them in turn to Charlie and Margaret and helping herself. One was set aside to cool for Floss.

The smell of fresh-cooked buttery potato-cake woke Wilson, as was to be expected. First his nose sipped the air, then his eyes opened, his gaze settled on the potato-cakes.

'Like one?' Alison asked.

Wilson opened his mouth wide and Alison put a potato-cake inside, whole.

'They're paradise-cakes,' Alison said.

'Potato-cakes?' said Wilson, recognizing the taste.

'No, paradise-cakes, Wilson,' and then, stepping aside, she gave him a clear view of Charlie's and Margaret's entertainment, with the umbrella and the sou'wester hat and his eiderdown. 'Look, Wilson, look.'

Wilson watched with wide-open eyes, and into his wide-open

mouth Alison put, one by one, the potato-cakes that were his share.

But, as they had foreseen, Wilson did not stay awake for very long. When there were no more potato-cakes, he yawned, drowsed, and suddenly was deeply asleep. Charlie and Margaret put him back into his eiderdown and took him upstairs to bed again. They came down to return the umbrella and the sou'wester to their proper places, and to see Floss back into her basket. Alison, last out of the kitchen, made sure that everything was in its place.

The next morning Mum was down first. On Sunday she always cooked a proper breakfast for anyone there in time. Dad was always there in time; but this morning Mum was still looking for a bowl of mashed potato when he appeared.

'I can't think where it's gone,' she said. 'I can't think.'

'I'll have the bacon and eggs without the potato,' said Dad; and he did. While he ate, Mum went back to searching.

Wilson came down, and was sent upstairs again to put on a dressing-gown. On his return he said that Charlie was still asleep and there was no sound from the girls' rooms either. He said he thought they were tired out. He went on talking while he ate his breakfast. Dad was reading the paper and Mum had gone back to poking about in the larder for the bowl of mashed potato, but Wilson liked talking even if no one would listen.

When Mum came out of the larder for a moment, still without her potato, Wilson was saying: '. . . and Charlie sat in an umbrella-boat on an eiderdown-sea, and Margaret pretended to be a sea-serpent, and Alison gave us paradise-cakes to eat. Floss had one too, but it was too hot for her. What are paradise-cakes? Dad, what's a paradise-cake?'

'Don't know,' said Dad, reading.

'Mum, what's a paradise-cake?'

'Oh, Wilson, don't bother so when I'm looking for something ... When did you eat this cake, anyway?'

'I told you. Charlie sat in his umbrella-boat on an eiderdown-sea and Margaret was a sea-serpent and Alison –'

'Wilson,' said his mother, 'you've been dreaming.'

'No, really – really!' Wilson cried.

But his mother paid no further attention. 'I give up,' she said. 'That mashed potato: it must have been last week-end ...' She went out of the kitchen to call the others: 'Charlie! Margaret! Alison!'

Wilson, in the kitchen, said to his father, 'I wasn't dreaming. And Charlie said there was a fly in his ear.'

Dad had been quarter-listening; now he put down his paper. 'What?'

'Charlie had a fly in his ear.'

Dad stared at Wilson. 'And what did you say that Alison fed you with?'

'Paradise-cakes. She'd just made them, I think, in the middle of the night.'

'What were they like?'

'Lovely. Hot, with butter. Lovely.'

'But were they – well, could they have had any mashed potato in them, for instance?'

In the hall Mum was finishing her calling: 'Charlie! Margaret! Alison! I warn you now!'

'I don't know about that,' Wilson said. 'They were paradise-cakes. They tasted a bit like the potato-cakes Mum makes, but Alison said they weren't. She specially said they were paradise-cakes.'

Dad nodded. 'You've finished your breakfast. Go up and get dressed, and you can take this' — he took a coin from his pocket – 'straight off to the sweetshop. Go on.'

Mum met Wilson at the kitchen door: 'Where's he off to in such a hurry?'

'I gave him something to buy sweets with,' said Dad. 'I wanted a quiet breakfast. He talks too much.'

PHILIPPA PEARCE

A Bunch of Flowers

It was my Mum's birthday and I decided to buy her a present like every year since last year (before that I was too little).

I took all the money out of my moneybox and luckily there was a lot because quite by chance Mum had given me some the day before. I knew what I was going to get her for a present: an enormous huge bunch of flowers to put in the big blue vase in the sitting-room.

I could hardly wait for school to be over so I could go and buy my present. I kept my hand in my pocket all the time at school so as not to lose my money, even when we were playing football at break – but since I wasn't in goal that didn't matter. Alec is our goalie. 'Why are you running about with one hand in your pocket?' he asked me. I explained that I was going to buy my Mum some flowers, and he said personally he'd rather have something to eat, like a cake or some sweets or sausage rolls, but since the present wasn't for him I took no notice and I got a ball past him into the goal. We won 44–32.

When we came out of school Alec went along to the flower shop with me, eating half the chocolate roll he'd saved from the grammar lesson. We went into the shop and I put all my money on the counter and told the lady I wanted an enormous huge bunch of flowers for my Mum, only no begonias because we had plenty of those in our garden, so it wasn't worth buying any more. 'We want something nice,' said Alec, and he went and stuck his nose into the flowers in the window to see how they smelt. The lady counted my money, and she said she was afraid she couldn't give me a *very* enormous bunch of flowers. I was very sad, so the lady looked at me and thought for a moment, and then she told me I was a dear little boy and she patted me on the head and said she'd fix it. She picked out all sorts of flowers, and she put in a lot of green leaves. Alec liked them, because he said they looked like nice fresh vegetables. It was a big bunch, really fantastic; the lady wrapped it up in crackly transparent paper and told me to be careful how I carried it. So now I had my big bunch of flowers and Alec had finished smelling the others in the window, and I said thank you to the lady and we went out.

I was feeling very pleased with my flowers when we met Geoffrey, Matthew and Rufus from school. 'Hey, look at Nicholas!' said Geoffrey. 'He looks a right twit with that bunch of flowers!' 'You're jolly lucky I'm carrying these flowers or I'd thump you!' I said. 'Give them to me,' said Alec. 'I don't mind holding them while you thump Geoffrey.' So I gave Alec my bunch of flowers, and Geoffrey thumped me. We had our fight, and then I said time was getting on, so we stopped. However, I had to wait a bit longer, because Matthew said, 'Just look at Alec – now *he* looks a right twit holding a bunch of flowers!' So Alec hit him over the head with the bunch of flowers. 'My flowers!' I shouted. 'You'll hurt my flowers!' I was right, too. Alec went on hitting Matthew with the bunch and the flowers were flying all over the place because the paper was torn, and Matthew was shouting, 'Doesn't hurt, yah boo, doesn't hurt!'

By the time Alec stopped Matthew's head was covered with

greenery and Alec was right, he did look like something you could cook for Sunday lunch. I started picking up my flowers and I told my friends they were beastly. 'That's right!' said Rufus. 'You shouldn't have gone and done that to Nicholas's flowers!' 'Nobody asked you!' said Geoffrey, and they started thumping each other. Alec had gone home, because the sight of Matthew's head made him feel hungry and he didn't want to be late for dinner.

I went off with my flowers. Some of them were missing, and there was no more greenery or paper left, but it was still a nice bunch. Then, a little further on, I met Eddie.

'Hi,' said Eddie, 'have a game of marbles?' 'I can't,' I said. 'I've got to get home and give my Mum these flowers.' But Eddie said it was still quite early. And I like playing marbles – I'm good at marbles, I just take aim and wham! I nearly always win. So I put my flowers down on the pavement and I started playing with Eddie, and it's great playing marbles with Eddie because he often loses. The trouble is he doesn't like losing and he said I was cheating and I told him he was lying, so he shoved me and I sat down on top of my bunch of flowers and it didn't do them any good. 'I'm going to tell Mum what you did to her flowers,' I said to Eddie, and Eddie was very upset. He helped me pick out the least squashed ones. I like Eddie, he's O.K.

I started off again. My bunch wasn't very big any more, but the flowers I did have left were all right; one of them was just a bit squashed, but the other two were fine. Then I saw Jeremy on his bike.

I decided I wasn't going to fight him, because if I went on fighting all my friends I met in the street I soon wouldn't have any flowers at all left to give Mum. Anyway, it's none of their business if I want to give my Mum some flowers. I've got a perfect right to give her flowers, and personally I think they're just jealous because Mum would be very pleased with me and give me something nice for pudding and tell me what a kind boy I am, so why do they all want to gang up on me anyway?

'Hi, Nicholas!' said Jeremy. 'Right twit yourself!' I shouted back. 'So what's the matter with my bunch of flowers, then?' Jeremy got off his bike and looked at me in surprise and said, 'What bunch of flowers?' 'This bunch of flowers!' I said, and I threw the flowers in his face. I don't think Jeremy was expecting to get a faceful of flowers, and anyway he didn't like it. He threw the flowers into the road and they landed on the roof of a passing car and drove off with the car. 'My flowers!' I shouted. 'My Mum's flowers!' 'Don't worry!' said Jeremy. 'I'll follow the car on my bike.' Jeremy's O.K, but he doesn't pedal very fast, specially not uphill, even if he says he *is* in training to win the Milk Race when he's grown up. When he came back he said he hadn't been able to catch up with the car, there was a lot of traffic and it had got away from him, but he did bring me back one flower which had fallen off its roof. Unfortunately it was the squashed one.

Jeremy rode off very fast – it's downhill all the way to his house – and I went home with my crumpled flower. I had a sort of a big lump in my throat. Like when I bring home my mark book with my monthly report and it's got all noughts in it.

I opened the door and I said, 'Happy birthday, Mum,' and then I burst into tears. Mum looked at the flower; she seemed a bit surprised. Then she put her arms round me and hugged me lots and lots of times, and she said it was the nicest bunch of flowers she'd ever had, and she put the flower in the big blue vase in the sitting-room.

I don't care what you say, my Mum is O.K!

RENÉ GOSCINNY

THE DRAGON WHO CHEATED

The kingdom of Urgburg-under-Ug was as pleasant a little place as you could wish to find. In fact, it was a great deal more pleasant than most people would dream of wishing to find. It was beautiful sunshiny summer all the year except on the 15th March when there was always a slight snowstorm.

But owing to a special arrangement that had something to do with leap years and that kind of thing, the 15th March occurred only twice in ten years in Urgburg-under-Ug.

Then again, the King and Queen of Urgburg-under-Ug were two exceedingly charming people, and about the only law that was ever enforced in the kingdom was one which said that no one was to be unhappy.

There was a special force of joyous policemen employed particularly to see that this law was not disobeyed. If anyone fell over and hurt himself, or dropped down a grating a penny that he was going to buy sweets with or anything like that, these joyous policemen would make funny faces and give them new pennies which the King secretly provided himself. That will just show you how nice it was in the kingdom of Urgburg.

There were only two things wrong with the kingdom of Urgburg-under-Ug.

One of them was its name which was slightly difficult to say and definitely difficult to spell, but that didn't matter very much because nobody minded whether it was pronounced properly or not except the Urgburg Broadcasting Company, and they knew how to pronounce it.

But there was a dragon in Urgburg, and a very unpleasant dragon at that. It arrived quite suddenly from goodness knows where and started stamping on places and burning things up with its fiery breath, and kicking things down with its spiky feet.

'This dragon business is most distressing,' said the King, who had gathered all his ministers together to discuss what should be done. 'What can we do to release the kingdom from such a monster?'

'Perfectly simple, my dear Gilbert,' said the Queen, who wasn't supposed to be at the conference at all. 'All you have to do is to issue a proclamation and say that you offer half the kingdom and the hand of the Princess in marriage to whoever shall slay the dragon.'

'But, my dear Agnes,' protested the King, 'you know perfectly well we haven't a princess.'

'Neither we have,' said the Queen; 'I was forgetting.'

She put her thumb in her mouth because it helped her to think, then remembering there was company present, if you can count ministers and chancellors as company, she hurriedly took it out again, and said, 'Well, we can still offer half the kingdom and there'd be sure to be plenty of nice strong dragon-slaying sort of people who would be willing to do a spot of work for a prize like that.'

'That's right enough,' said the King; 'they might even be more willing to slay the dragon for half the kingdom alone than if they thought they had to marry a princess as well. I don't suppose all dragon-slaying people are very used to princesses, and it might put them out a bit. You know what I mean – having to turn half a kingdom into a little kingdom of its own and be majestic sort of majesties themselves, so that the Princess should not feel homesick.'

'That's what I think,' put in the Prime Minister. 'I know a man who has a sister who used to know a friend who once heard of a dragon-slaying sort of man who slew a dragon to win half a kingdom and a princess, and he used to say –'

'Now never mind what he used to say,' broke in the Queen

hurriedly, guessing that whatever it was it would take a long time to tell because she used to say things like that to her friends and it used to take her ages. 'Let's think out the proclamation.'

'Certainly, my dear,' said the King, licking his pencil which was copying-ink, only he had forgotten, and it made his tongue all purple. 'Let me see, how does this sound? "Wanted, superior dragon-slayer"...'

'No, no,' said the Queen, 'don't say "superior". It doesn't matter what sort of a dragon-slayer he is so long as he slays the dragon.'

'Pardon me, Majesties,' put in the Lord High Marshal of Heralds, who knew all about proclamations because he used to be a herald in another kingdom before he came to Urgburg, and had shouted many a one round the streets. 'Pardon me, but if I might make so bold as to say so, proclamations ought to start with "Oyez".'

'Oyez,' said the King.

'Oh! no,' said the Queen, 'that is much too old-fashioned. We must be up-to-date.'

'Dragons are rather old-fashioned,' put in the Prime Minister, who had not quite forgiven the Queen for stopping him from telling them about the man that his friend's sister's acquaintance had heard of, and thought this was a chance to get his own back. But by this time the King, who had been writing away like anything on the back of an old piece of paper for several minutes, suddenly said, 'Listen to this. "Oyez, oyez – wanted, dragon-slayer to slay dragon" – that doesn't sound quite right, but I can't think of any other way of saying it – "half kingdom reward, no princess, no questions asked."'

At this, there was a tremendous babble of voices, as everybody started talking at once and saying how they thought the proclamation ought to go, and the noise became so loud that the King had to go outside and have a cannon or two let off to get silence.

'Now, I'll tell you what we'll do,' said the Queen; 'everyone is to go away and write out in nice clear handwriting their own idea of a proclamation. Then we shall all meet again here at this time tomorrow and there'll be a small prize for the one whose proclamation is considered the best.'

Everybody applauded this idea except the King, who guessed that he would have to pay for the little present, but before he could say anything, the tea bell rang, and everybody streamed out, headed by the Queen, who was rather good at that sort of thing.

Next day, at the appointed time, the proclamations were read out.

The Lord Chancellor had written his in rhyme, because he liked to think he was rather a poet, although nobody else could bear to think it.

'Oyez, oyez, and be it known
A dragon-slayer's needed
To free the kingdom, save the throne,
So let this call be heeded.
And as reward for such as can
This monster overthrow,
One-half this land Elysian
Shall to the slayer go.'

'What does "Elysian" mean?' asked the King, who had an aunt named Elizabeth Ann, and thought it might have something to do with her and didn't want to get aunts mixed up with state affairs.

'I don't like "such as can",' said the Queen, 'and anyway, who said a proclamation had to rhyme? Next, please.'

'Oyez, oyez,' began the Prime Minister, then feeling that he had done quite well so far, he went on in a louder voice, 'slay the dragon and win a handsome prize. Half the kingdom for a successful attempt. No entrance fee, no difficulties. Their Majesties' decision is final.'

'That sounds as if a dragon was a sort of crossword puzzle,' said the Queen, who didn't hold with crossword puzzles because the King could do them better than she could. 'Next, please.'

This was the Lord High Marshal of Heralds. He popped up very quickly and in a voice that could be heard all over the place read out:

'Oyez, oyez, oyez. Whereas the Kingdom of Urgburg-under-Ug is suffering under the onslaughts of a dragon, be it known that we by our royal privilege do hereby offer half the said kingdom, together with all the appurtenances thereof, as prize or reward to whomsoever shall slay the monster. Given under our hand this so and so day.'

Of course that was by far the best attempt of any, but the King said he thought the Lord High Marshal of Heralds knew too much about proclamations.

Then the rest of them had a go at reading out their attempts except two of the ministers who had not been able to get any further than chewing the end of a pencil, and one who had been looking over the Lord Chancellor's shoulder, but hadn't been able to read his writing.

'Well,' said the Queen, rather briskly. 'I did one myself.' She read out:

'Oyez, oyez. We have had the most terrible dragon ravishing the kingdom lately, and what do you think it's been doing? I mean to say, too devastating, you know. Why, my dears, positively stamping on places and all that. Something must be done about it, so the King and myself thought that if we could get someone to slay the dragon, because we feel sure that nobody really likes the nasty thing, we would give him half the kingdom for his trouble. So –'

'Here, here,' broke in the King.

'Don't applaud until I've finished,' said the Queen, thinking he meant an applauding sort of thing like 'Hear, hear!'

'But you can't have a proclamation like that,' said the King.

Then the King and Queen started arguing, partly about the proclamation but very much more so about the small prize, chiefly because the Queen's idea of a small prize was a very big one.

'I tell you what we'll do,' said the King at last, 'you shall have a nice diamond necklace for your prize for the proclamation, but we'll use the Lord High Marshal of Heralds' proclamation because it sounds better.'

'All right,' replied the Queen, who didn't mind so long as she got the prize, and as nobody else minded either because the King promised them all consolation prizes, the matter was settled.

But although the proclamation was settled, the dragon wasn't, and next day news came that he had kicked down two more castles.

The dragon sat at the mouth of his cave cleaning his claws with a tree-trunk.

'Huh! Huh!' he growled, 'so they want to get me killed, do they? I'll teach them to send out proclamations. I'll teach them a thing or two about killing dragons.'

He had heard the proclamation read out because he had rather good ears and four of them at that, two on each of his two heads.

'Disgraceful, I call it,' said one head.

'I've got an idea,' said the other.

'Well, out with it,' said the first.

'Psp, psp,' said the other, trying to whisper.

'What say?' said the first head.

'Get suit of armour, disguise self as champion, pretend kill own self, claim half kingdom as reward.'

'Good idea, but don't talk like telegram,' said the first head, talking like one itself.

The dragon shook one head and nodded the other, and went round to one of the castles he had kicked down and rummaged about to find some armour. He had a very severe portion of trouble getting himself into the armour, partly because his tail was rather

long and he had to wind it round himself which made him rather fat, and partly because he had to get both his heads into one helmet.

'They say two heads are better than one,' said the first head.

'I can't see it myself,' said the second.

'Move over a bit,' said the first.

At last the dragon got himself all fastened up by using about four-and-a-half suits of armour to cover him, and set out for the King's palace.

'Majesty,' he said, bowing before the throne as he was ushered into the King's presence, 'I come as your champion. I will kill the dragon if you promise me the reward you have offered.' He said this with both his heads at once, so it sounded nice and loud even though the visor of his helmet was down so that no one could see he was really the dragon himself.

'Ask him to open his hat,' said the Queen, who was not used to people talking through their helmets at her, although she used to say that some of the ministers talked through their hats, but that, of course, was a different thing.

'Shush,' whispered the King, 'you may upset him, and look what a nice big champion he is. No dragon will stand a chance against such a whopper.' Then aloud he said, 'Certainly, go and slay the dragon, bring back proof that you have slain it and half the kingdom shall be yours.'

'Majesty,' boomed the dragon's two heads, 'it shall be done.'

And with a clatter and clang of all four-and-a-half suits of armour, he strode out of the palace with such a swish that all the blinds came down and three of the ministers thought it was night-time and went to bed.

Once again the dragon was sitting outside his cave, but this time he wasn't cleaning his claws. He was very carefully cutting a circular piece out of the side of a large tray. Then he put the tray on his shoulder with the cut-out piece round one of his necks, held it there with one paw, put his other head on one side, and looked at his reflection in the pond.

'Excellent,' said the first head.

'Looks just as if you are carrying the dragon's head on a tray,' said the second head.

'Entirely satisfactory,' said both heads together.

The dragon put his helmet on again, putting it on to one head only this time, and back he went to the palace. He strode up the throne-room, making the windows rattle as he went. He held the head on which he wore the helmet slightly on one side and he kept the eyes on his other head closed, and as he held the tray on his shoulder, it looked for all the world as if he was a mighty champion bearing the head of the slain dragon on the tray.

Cheers went up as he went by.

'Hoorah for the dragon-slayer! Hail champion of Urgburg-under-Ug! The dragon is slain!'

'Majesty,' said the dragon, being careful to talk only with the

head that was inside the helmet, 'I have slain the dragon. See, I bring his head as proof. I come to claim my reward of half the kingdom.'

'Lovely,' said the Queen, clapping her hands. 'What a horrid-looking dragon it was.'

'Terrible,' said the King.

And the dragon who didn't know whether he wanted to laugh because his plan was succeeding so well, or to be angry because they were saying such rude things about him, but who knew he mustn't do either until he got his reward, passed round the throne-room, pretending to show off the head on the tray.

Oh! dreadful situation, think of it! The dragon about to be given half the kingdom for slaying himself! Not that it would have mattered if he had slain himself, but of course he hadn't. He was tricking the King. He was tricking the entire kingdom. When he had got half the kingdom for himself he would still go on ravaging the other half. Instead of Urgburg-under-Ug being delivered from the dragon, it would be delivered to the dragon. Everything would be terrible. Oh! crafty monster! Oh! to think that nothing could be done to save the kingdom!

The King stood up.

'According to the terms of the proclamation,' he cried, 'I have much pleasure in presenting to our valiant champion one-half of the kingdom of Urgburg-under-Ug.' Then, turning to the disguised dragon, 'Won't you put the head down, sir, and take a cup of wine?'

'Oo-er,' thought the dragon, 'can't put my own head down. I'd better pretend to be a bit dashing.' Then aloud:

'Majesty, I prefer to keep the head of this monster as a trophy.'

The Queen was just going to ask what a trophy was, when from amongst the spectators a young man pushed his way forward, and ran towards the dragon.

'Go back,' cried the King, 'go away.'

But the young man didn't go back or away. He ran forward with a small bright object clasped firmly in his hand. It was a pepper-box. He shook its contents on to the tray in front of the dragon's head.

'Arrest him,' roared the King.

The guards had taken hardly a step when –

'ATISHOO!' A most frightfully monstrous noise rang out. The head of the supposed-to-be-slain dragon had sneezed!

Pandemonium raged. The cheers that had gone up before gave place to screams of fear and howls of alarm. The King jumped up so suddenly that he kicked the throne over backwards and the Queen with it, but happily she fell on some cushions.

'He is no champion,' said the young man, pointing to the dragon who had torn the helmet off his other head and was beginning to puff out sparks, 'he is the dragon himself.'

'Huh, huh,' roared the dragon in a voice that blew all the guards' hats off in a shower. 'Yes, I am the dragon and I will have not half the kingdom but all of it. It's just my dinner-time – what a meal I'll have!' He rolled his eyes round the throne-room and blew out a jet of blue flame.

Forty-seven duchesses fainted all at once. The Lord Chamberlain climbed up on the chandelier, the Prime Minister and the Lord Chief Justice tried to get up the chimney but got stuck half-way.

The dragon advanced, a terrifying form, upon the young man.

'Have at ye!' cried the young man, who had read in a book that champions always said that when attacking the foe. He drew his sword with a flourish. Horrors! the blade flew off the handle. Urgburg-under-Ug was undone! The last hope was gone. No, it wasn't! Marvels of all marvels! The shining sword blade flew like a streak of silver across the room and through both the dragon's heads at once, skewering them like an enormous pennyworth of cat's meat.

With a sensational crash that shook all the pictures down in the Queen's spare bedroom, the dragon fell lifeless to the floor. Serve him right for cheating. The pieces of armour from his four-and-a-half suits rolled and clanged all over the place like so many milk-churns or even more.

More cheers went up. Forty-six of the fainted duchesses came unfainted again and asked for cups of tea. The Queen climbed out of the cushions and helped the King stand the throne up again. The Lord Chamberlain dropped off the chandelier with a loud 'bong' into the middle of the floor, but didn't hurt himself much as he wore thick trousers. The Prime Minister and the Lord Chief Justice came out of the chimney followed by a large helping of soot.

The kingdom of Urgburg-under-Ug was saved!

'But tell me,' said the King to the young man, when they were sitting down to a nice banquet to celebrate the great occasion, 'who are you and how did you guess the dragon's trick?'

'I am Prince Diddinott Dottimwun,' said the young man. 'My kingdom which is near here was stamped out of existence by the dragon the Thursday before last. I followed him and saw him preparing to trick you into giving him half your kingdom.'

'Splendid,' said the King, 'now you can have half of my kingdom, and marry the Princess, and everything will be all lovely.'

'Shush,' said the Queen, 'we haven't got a princess. You said so yourself.'

'Neither we have!' exclaimed the King, it being his turn to look rather silly.

'Never mind,' said the young man, 'everything is quite all right. I never did care much for girls, anyway.'

So the Prince ruled over half the kingdom of Urgburg-under-Ug, but whether he cared much for girls anyway, or not, it wasn't very long before he fell in love with a rather special young duchess. So this rather unlikely sort of story comes to a nice usual sort of end because they were married and lived happily ever after.

NORMAN HUNTER

The Snowtime Express

The snow came down all through the night.

Down, down, down – all through the quiet night.

In the morning, when Jonny woke up, he looked out of his window.

The whole world was white.

'Yipee!' cried Jonny. 'Where's my sled?'

Across the street, Carol looked out of her window.

What a surprise!

Carol had never seen so much snow.

'Hurray!' cried Carol. 'Where's my sled?'

Mothers and fathers were busy looking out of windows, too.

Up and down the street, they were looking out at the snow.

But the fathers didn't say, 'Yipee!'

No indeed.

They shook their heads and said, 'No cars today! It will be hard to get to work!'

The mothers did not say, 'Hooray!'

The mothers were thinking, 'Mr Vick will not be able to send us any food from his store.'

Mrs Nally lived next door to Jonny.

She had a little baby.

'Oh, dear,' said Mrs Nally. 'How will I get a box of baby food for little Tommy?'

Mrs Dorman lived next door to Mrs Nally.

She was taking care of two little grandchildren.

'Oh dear,' said Mrs Dorman. 'Not a bit of bread in the house today! How can I get some bread?'

Down the street lived old Mrs Green.

She was very old.

It was hard for her to walk.

She looked out at the snow and said, 'Oh, dear! I did so want some cheese for my lunch today.'

Jonny was the first one out with his sled.

Then Carol came out with hers.

She came slowly through the deep snow to play with Jonny.

First they pulled each other on the sleds.

Then they tried to run with their sleds and get a ride.

Then they tied the two sleds together and played they had a sled train.

Soon Jonny's mother came out.

'Jonny,' she said. 'Do you think you could get all the way down the street to the store? We need some lunch meat today, and Mr Vick can't send it.'

Jonny looked down the street. How deep the snow was!

'I don't know,' he said.

'Maybe you can go on your sled train,' said his mother.

Jonny looked at Carol.

Carol looked at Jonny.

'Yipee!' cried Jonny. 'Let's go! Here comes the Snowtime Express!'

And off they went.

'Let's make stops, like a train,' said Carol.

So they made a stop.

They rang Mrs Nally's bell.

'Snowtime Express going to Mr Vick's,' said Jonny. 'Do you want us to bring anything for you?'

'Oh, yes, yes!' said Mrs Nally. 'Please bring me some baby food for little Tommy.'

'Toot! Toot!' said Jonny, and the sled train went on its way.

'Let's make another stop,' said Carol.

So they made another stop.

They rang Mrs Dorman's bell.

'Snowtime Express going to Mr Vick's,' said Carol. 'Do you want us to bring anything?'

'Oh, yes,' said Mrs Dorman. 'Please bring me some bread.'

'Toot! Toot!' said Jonny. 'All aboard!'

And the sled train went on its way.

'Let's make one more stop,' said Carol.

So they made one more stop.

They rang old Mrs Green's bell.

'Snowtime Express going to Mr Vick's,' said Jonny. 'Do you want us to bring anything back for you?'

'Oh, yes, yes,' said Mrs Green. 'Please bring me some yellow cheese.'

Toot! Toot!

The Snowtime Express went on its way to the store.

It had to go slower and slower as it got down the street.

Carol and Jonny took turns pulling and pushing.

Sometimes the sled train got stuck in the snow.

One time Jonny had to pull and pull. He gave a hard pull, and Carol tumbled right into the snow.

The sled train stuck again near the store.

This time it was Carol who pulled. She pulled and pulled. Then she went on.

But where was Jonny?

Sitting in the snow!

'Wait for me!' cried Jonny.

At last they got to the store.

'Toot! Toot!' they cried. 'Here comes the Snowtime Express!'

What a surprise for Mr Vick!

'Well, well,' he said. 'A sled train is just what we need today.'

He got a box and tied it on the sled.

Into the box went the baby food, and the bread, the cheese and the meat.

'There,' said Mr Vick. 'You can take out one thing at a time. The box will stay on your train.'

'All aboard!' cried Jonny.

'All aboard!' cried Carol.

And the Snowtime Express started back.

Slowly, slowly, the sled train made its way back up the street.

First Carol pulled and Jonny pushed. 'Toot! Toot! Clear the track!' cried Carol.

Then Jonny pulled and Carol pushed. 'Out of the way for the Snowtime Express!' cried Jonny.

It was hard work, but lots of fun.

'Toot! Toot!' cried Carol. 'First stop at Mrs Green's.'

How happy Mrs Green was to get her yellow cheese!

'Thank you,' she said. 'That's the best train running today.'

Toot! Toot!

The next stop was at Mrs Dorman's.

How glad she was to get the bread!

Then the train stopped at the Nally house.

'Thank you, Snowtime Express,' said Mrs Nally. 'Now little Tommy will have a good lunch.'

The last stop was at Jonny's house. He ran in and gave his mother the lunch meat.

When he came out again Carol said, 'Look, Jonny!'

In the box on the sled train was a white paper bag.

'Say, what's this?' asked Jonny. 'We made all our stops, didn't we?'

'Yes,' said Carol; 'I guess Mr Vick made a mistake.'

But it was no mistake.

Carol and Jonny opened the bag.

There were two lollipops in it!

Two big lollipops!

The red one said, 'For Carol'.

The green one said, 'For Jonny'.

So Carol and Jonny sat down on the Snowtime Express, and they ate their lollipops right then and there!

LILIAN MOORE

JACK JACKDAW

I must tell you about Jack. Jack won't like it. He'll squawk and fluff out his black feathers in a huff, but he's our school bird and we're proud of him – even if he is rather bad-tempered.

I first met Jack on the day I started school. He was walking up and down on the wall at the end of the playground during morning break.

I was standing by the wall because I didn't like the big wide space in the middle of the playground. For a while I watched this strange black bird with a grey head and then I said.

'Hello, birdie. Pretty birdie.'

Jack looked at me with a beady eye and said 'Jack-Jackdaw,' very clearly.

A boy was standing beside me.

'He's not pretty,' the boy said. 'Do you like birds? I like birds. My Grannie's got a budgie that can talk.'

That boy was my first friend at school. He still is my friend too. He's called Robert and I'm called Sarah.

After that Robert and I always went to talk to Jack if he was perched on the wall. Sometimes he made a lot of noise.

'Jack-Jack-Jack-Jackdaw,' he would squawk. Then he would laugh and whistle and make a funny hubbub noise like a lot of children in a distant playground.

But at other times he would not talk at all, even though the whole class would try to make him. He would walk and hop along the wall opening his beak at us and wagging his head.

We asked our teacher, Mrs Stacey, about Jack.

'Now, let me think,' she said. 'He's a jackdaw, you know. And he's been around the school for a couple of months now. He seems so tame that the headmistress thought he might be someone's pet. We put a notice about him in the village post office. But nobody claimed him. I don't suppose anybody wanted him. He isn't a pretty sight, is he? All those scrawny grey feathers standing up on his head.'

Robert and Mrs Stacey were right. Jack was not a pretty bird.

His feathers standing up in spikes made him look as if he was always cross about something. And the way he squawked wasn't very appealing either. Some of the children said they were frightened of him. But I don't think they were really. Although he sounded fierce, he never pecked anybody.

He used to eat out of the pig bins which stood in a row near the school kitchens. All the scraps which didn't get eaten at dinner time used to go in those pig bins. Sometimes Robert and I picked up the lids to look inside because it was so horrible. We saw mashed potato and gravy and vegetables all mixed up with custard and lumps of pudding. It really looked disgusting. Jack loved it. He used to walk up and down nearby pretending to think of other things. Then, if a lid was left a bit askew, he would flap up on to the edge of a bin, grab a piece of pastry or half a fish finger, and make off to the top of the games shed to eat it.

While he ate it he would jump and flap and bash his food on the shed roof. He made rather a mess of the roof and Mr Hudson, the school caretaker, didn't like him at all.

But Robert and I liked Jack more and more. We looked for him every morning when we arrived at school, and we said good-bye to him if he was around when it was time to go home.

And Jack began to like us.

Robert and I spent a year in Mrs Stacey's class. After a while we got used to the big empty playground and played in the middle of it as well as by the wall. And after a while Jack got used to it too. He flapped around Robert saying 'Aark-aark', and tried to join in our games. He particularly liked skipping. As soon as he saw a rope he would bob up and down as if he were jumping over it. Robert tried to teach him some skipping rhymes.

'Come on, Jack,' Robert used to say. 'I like coffee. I like tea. I like Jackdaw in with me.'

But Jack used to turn and walk off, hunching his shoulders.

'Jack-Jack-Jackdaw,' he would say looking back at Robert.

'Perhaps he's too old to learn new words,' said Robert.

But Robert was wrong. Jack was taking things in all right. And he began to make himself unpopular.

Our headmistress was a kind lady and always said good morning to the children in the playground when she arrived at school each day. Usually she said 'Good morning, Robert,' or 'Good morning, Sarah,' because she knew all our names. But sometimes she said 'Good morning, dear,' if she wasn't thinking of names just then, and Jack picked it up.

One morning the headmistress walked in at the school gate and Jack was waiting for her on the wall.

'Good morning, dear,' said Jack loudly in exactly the headmistress's voice.

The headmistress looked very surprised but she laughed.

'You saucy bird, Jack,' she said and walked on across the playground.

Jack flopped down on to the ground and hobbled after her.

'Good morning, dear. Good morning, dear. Good morning, dear,' he said.

'Yes, Jack. I heard you the first time,' said the headmistress as she went into the school.

But Jack didn't take the hint. He carried on saying 'Good morning, dear' to the headmistress every time he saw her. And I could see she got tired of it.

There were a lot of children in our school but Robert was the one Jack liked best. Robert used to bring him little tit-bits from home. Once he even brought him some of his seventh-birthday cake. Robert put it down on the ground for Jack to peck. Jack squawked and tossed bits of cake in the air, laughing in a cackling voice as he did so.

'You've got no manners, Jack,' said Robert.

'Aark-aark,' said Jack happily.

Not long after that Robert was made goal-keeper for the school football team. Jack liked that. He was able to perch on the crossbar of the football goal and keep Robert company. Whenever the ball came anywhere near the goal Jack used to flap and squawk and nearly fall off his bar with excitement. Robert said it was encouraging to have such a noisy fan. But the sports master said Jack was a 'plaguey nuisance'.

One day a team from the school in the next village came to play our school at football. I was able to watch, although I hadn't been chosen for the team.

A boy from the other school team saw Jack flap across the football pitch and land on the goalpost.

'Look at that old crow,' he shouted.

'That's a jackdaw,' I shouted back at him. 'He's our mascot. He brings us luck.'

And Jack did bring us luck. The visiting team were very good footballers and the ball kept coming dangerously close to Robert's goal. But Jack flapped and yelled and kept distracting the players so that Robert was able to get the ball each time it was kicked towards the goal. But at half time the teams changed ends and Robert went off down the pitch to defend the other goal. Jack decided to stay put. He perched above the other goal-keeper's head and peered down at him. Then he opened his beak and gaped at him. And just as one of our players was about to kick the ball hard into the goal Jack said 'Good morning, dear' to the goal-keeper, and the ball slammed into the back of the net.

We all cheered and jumped and clapped. Jack squawked and flew off towards the school.

'It's that old crow,' shouted the goal-keeper. 'He distracted me. He did. He did it on purpose.'

The sports master from the visiting school looked very annoyed.

'I'm sorry about that jackdaw,' said our sports teacher. 'He's becoming a plaguey nuisance around the school. He won't leave us alone.'

Have you ever heard stories about magpies and jackdaws stealing things? Well, it's true. It isn't that they are dishonest or anything like that. They just like collecting things, especially shiny things.

Jack was always on the look-out for something new to add to his collection. The litter bin in the school playground was filled with bits of tin-foil wrappings from sweets and biscuits. Jack used to sort out the bin, hurling any litter he didn't want on the ground.

'That bird makes this school look like a slum,' Mr Hudson, the caretaker, used to say as he cleared up after Jack.

For a while we wondered what Jack did with all his bits of foil and rubbish. Then Mr Hudson found out. Jack stuffed them down the narrow gap between the games shed and the wall of the school. He must have been doing it for months, perhaps even for years. The gap was almost filled up with rubbish and Mr Hudson spent hours pulling it all out with a pair of tongs on a long stick.

'I'll wring that bird's neck if I get half the chance,' I heard him mutter.

Robert and I were beginning to worry about Jack being in so much trouble. Several of the teachers thought he was nothing but a nuisance. Then he made matters worse by trying to visit Robert in school.

We were in Mr Maynard's class when Jack dropped in on Robert one morning. We had been set some geography work to get on with when suddenly Jack flap-flapped in at an open window of the classroom and landed with a flump and a squawk on Robert's exercise book. He lay there for a moment with his beak open as if the drop had been further than he expected. Then he stood up,

shook himself a little, and said, 'Good morning, dear,' to Mr Maynard.

Mr Maynard was not pleased. He could see what a muddy mess Jack had made of Robert's geography book.

'Get that bird out of here Robert,' he said crossly.

'Sorry, Mr Maynard,' said Robert as if he had invited Jack to come and ruin his work. 'I'll take him out.'

But Jack had a different plan. He jumped down on to the floor and hopped around under the desks squawking and grumbling. Luckily he spotted a metal pencil sharpener which somebody had dropped on the floor and he began to pick this up in his beak and hurl it about. This gave Robert a chance to grab him and carry him out. Strangely enough, Jack seemed to like being held by Robert and he gave a chirpy sound. But then he caught sight of Mr Maynard and said 'Aark-aark' in a cross voice.

'Aark-aark yourself,' said Mr Maynard. 'And don't come back.'

Half an hour later Jack came back.

There was a scratching at the door leading out to the big school corridor. Mr Maynard opened the door to see what the noise was.

'Good morning, dear – Aark,' said Jack, standing up very straight with all his head feathers standing up straight as well.

All the class roared with laughter and Jack laughed too in a screaming, showing-off sort of voice which made Mr Maynard furious.

'Robert,' he said, 'get that fowl out of here and shut the school door. And tell him that if he comes in again I'll wring his neck.'

'The teachers don't like Jack,' said Robert as we went home that evening.

'Do you think Mr Maynard would really wring his neck?' I asked.

'No,' said Robert. 'But I know Mr Hudson wants to get rid of him.'

'How will they do it?' I asked.

'I don't know,' said Robert. 'But I think we ought to get Jack away from school for a while.'

Two evenings later we had a plan to save Jack. We didn't tell anyone else. But when we were going home we searched for Jack and found him perched on top of the games shed.

'Good morning, dear,' he said to Robert in a friendly way. So Robert clambered up on to my shoulders and tried to grab him. But he didn't have to. Jack walked on to his arm and made those chirpy noises he had done in the classroom.

Robert was delighted, although it was difficult to climb down again without letting go of Jack.

Then we had to run home because we were late and our mothers might have been worried. Jack was jolted rather a lot and looked more beady-eyed than usual by the time we reached my house. We just had time to push him under our garage door and shut it down before Robert had to run off home.

A little while later Robert came back with some biscuits and an apple for Jack.

'We must give Jack some food,' he said. 'Then he'll like it here and stay.'

So I took some of the chocolate cake I had had for my tea and we went to the garage.

Very carefully we pulled up the swing door and crept inside.

'Jack,' we whispered. 'Here's your tea.'

'Come on, Jack. Where are you?' said Robert.

Then we both saw the open window. We had forgotten about the window. Usually it was shut. But this evening it was open and Jack had gone.

We searched the garden. We searched the trees down the road. We went all the way back to the school. But Jack was nowhere. He had vanished. And it was all our fault.

'I expect he'll turn up at school tomorrow,' said Robert as he went back home that evening.

'I hope so,' I said.

But Jack didn't turn up. Every day Robert and I searched for him. We asked Mr Hudson if he had seen him, but he said, 'No. And good riddance. I reckon.'

We asked Mrs Stacey and all the teachers who hadn't minded Jack too much. But nobody had seen him.

We felt terrible. The football team wondered where their mascot was and Robert kept letting balls into the goal. We looked hopefully at every passing rook or crow that flew overhead, but it was never Jack.

I told my mother what I had done and how sorry I was. She was very kind and said she was sure Jack could look after himself. She also said the village school was better off without him. But I didn't really agree with that.

All that happened two years ago. Since then there has been no sign of Jack. No sign, that is, until yesterday morning.

You see, Robert and I started at our new school in town yesterday. We had to go in on a school bus with lots of other children from our village. The new school has green railings along the front on to the main road where the buses stop.

As we got off the bus Robert grabbed my arm and pointed. Way down the road at the very end of the railings was a small black hunched figure.

'Aark,' it said as we ran up the road. 'Good morning, dear.'

'JACK JACKDAW,' yelled Robert. 'It is. It really is JACK.'

I think I have never been so happy. And Jack was happy too.

He flapped and bowed and squawked before jumping clumsily on to Robert's shoulder and rubbing his beak against his ear.

Robert walked into school with Jack still perched on his shoulder. A teacher came out of the main door.

'Don't bring that bird into school,' said the teacher. 'He's a terrible nuisance. He's become the school mascot and lives in a heap of rubbish behind the bicycle sheds. We wouldn't be without him now. But *not* inside the school buildings, you understand.'

So Robert put Jack gently down on the grass in front of the school.

'It's nice to see a friendly face in a new school,' said Robert, blowing his nose because he was so pleased.

'Aark-aark,' said Jack, and waddled off around the corner.

'I expect he's going to the pig bins,' I said happily.

In the afternoon Robert told our new teacher about Jack's story. He was very interested and said he would tell the local newspaper about it. So a photographer came to the school this morning to take Jack's picture. Jack was on the railings preening himself when the photographer came up to him and held up his camera to take a picture.

'Aark,' said Jack and swooped down to take a close look at the camera. It was just the sort of thing Jack likes for his load-of-rubbish collection. But the photographer was alarmed and flapped his arm at Jack to keep him away.

'Good morning, dear,' said Jack and flew away over the school, as if he had more important things to do.

'Bother,' said our teacher, 'I was thinking of getting the regional television people to come and film him too.'

But Jack isn't the sort of bird to sit nicely for cameras. So I thought I had better write down his story and you could see what he's like from the drawings.

ANNE ROOKE

EGGS

'Oh, how I wish I had an alarm clock,' sighed Mrs Smith each morning. 'Every single day little Sam is late for school, and William is late for work.'

William, her husband, took no notice of this. He was spraying his roses. Nothing but roses grew in Mr Smith's garden, which lay right by the road. People walking along could lean over the low wooden fence and breathe in the scent, which was like warm Madeira cake mixed with raspberry trifle. And they could gaze at the gorgeous colours of flowers, red, white, pink, flame, yellow, and orange. People walked very slowly along that stretch of road. Bees hummed among the roses all day; they came from all over the country to make honey from Mr Smith's roses. And from March to November Mr Smith spent every free hour in his garden, watering, digging, raking the ground, picking off dead flowers, pruning, and spraying the roses and plants to get rid of greenfly, caterpillars, and nibbling insects.

There wasn't any room for little Sam in the garden. *He* had to play on the cement strip by the back door. And he would have liked a kitten, or maybe a puppy, but his father said animals would damage the flowers.

Every day little Sam was late for school because his father, who drove him there, had to be called in from the garden where he was caring for his roses; and every day Mr Smith was late for his job in the garden shop where he worked, selling roses and mowers and wheelbarrows.

Mr Smith liked working in the garden shop because he could get rose plants at half price.

'Hurry, William!' cried his wife. 'You'll be late! And Sam will be late for school. Here're your sandwiches, Sam, and your school bag. And, William, will you *please* buy me an alarm clock, so we can all get up earlier in the morning?'

'If I remember,' said Mr Smith. But she knew he would not remember. He would just buy another rose plant.

Father and son were leaving by the back door, to get to the shed where Mr Smith kept his old pick-up, when, guess what happened! With a crash louder than eighty tons of boulders falling on an ice rink, a lorry skidded off the road – across the pavement – through the wooden fence – and straight into Mr Smith's garden, ploughing over the roses, and ending up with its radiator jammed into the next-door fence. Then it fell on its side, because Mr Smith's garden was on quite a steep slope.

If Mr Smith had stayed in his garden *one minute* longer, *he* would have been run over too, along with his roses!

'Mercy!' cried Mrs Smith, running out of the back door. '*Mercy*, what's happened? Sam! William! Are you all right?'

'Oh, my lord! Oh, my roses!' wailed Mr Smith.

For the roses that had not been mashed by the truck were now completely buried under its load, which had tumbled out all over the garden.

What was that load?

Eggs! The truck had been taking forty thousand eggs to a cake factory. And every single one was now lying smashed all over Mr Smith's rose bed.

'What *happened?*' Mrs Smith asked the driver, who had clambered down, gulping and trembling, from his cab.

'A bee stung me, that's what! Made me swerve.'

'I'll want compensation for this,' moaned Mr Smith, looking at his ruined rose-bed. 'Compensation! My roses would have taken all the prizes at the County Show tomorrow.'

'My firm will pay you,' said the driver.

'Maybe we can buy an alarm clock with the money,' said Mrs Smith. But she didn't really believe so. She knew the money would go to buy more rose plants. 'Look at all those broken eggs! Not a whole one among them. What a shame! What a waste!'

The garden was bright yellow, and all gooey. Little Sam was up to his knees in egg yolk.

'Sam, come out of that! *Look* at you!'

But Sam called, 'Hey, Ma, look what I found! One egg isn't broken. Just one! Can I have it?' he asked the driver, who was limping indoors to phone for the breakdown service.

'Help yourself, son. No one's going to count those eggs . . .'

As Sam gently held the egg in his hand, he felt something alive, moving about inside it.

'Oh! It made a noise! There's a live chick in there! Ma, can I keep it? Can I hatch it?'

'Dad doesn't want chickens in the garden,' began Mrs Smith. But then she looked at the ruined roses and said, 'Oh, what's the difference? Put it in a basket by the stove where it'll keep warm. Now, clean yourself up for school. I never did *see* such a sight –'

'Egg yolks must be good for the ground,' sighed Mr Smith.

When little Sam came home at tea time, the egg in the basket was beginning to bump and joggle about. And then, crack! It opened. Out crawled a damp and yellow chick.

'Give it a spoonful of cereal,' said Sam's mother. 'And a drink of water.'

Soon the chick was dry, and yellow and fluffy.

'I'll call him Herbert,' said Sam.

'Perhaps it's a hen,' said his mother.

But Herbert was a cock. Long before Mr Smith had dug in the broken eggshells, and before the new roses were planted and blooming, Herbert had grown into a splendid rooster. He had a scarlet comb, black and green tail feathers, a gold-brown chest, and orange legs with black feather breeches. He followed Sam everywhere, sat beside him on the new patch of grass that had been planted, and ate all the slugs and snails in the garden.

And, every morning, sharp at half-past six, he shouted:

'Cock-a-doodle-doo! Time to get up! Cock-a-doodle-doo!'

Never again did Mrs Smith need to wish for an alarm clock. Or Sam for a kitten.

JOAN AIKEN

The Paper Palace

Caroline had a bad leg and it kept her in bed for a long time. She was fearfully bored, because she had read all her books and used up all her paints.

Then her grandmother bought her a present. A nice present: a pair of scissors.

'For my nails?' asked Caroline.

'No,' said Grandmother. 'To cut things out of paper.'

'What kind of things?' asked Caroline.

'People,' said Grandmother. 'And animals and trees and houses and anything you can think of.'

It was not at all easy. First Caroline cut out a car, but it looked more like a jam jar on legs. Then she made a hare and a rabbit, but they looked more like funny hats.

She took a new sheet of paper and cut out another animal.

'Did *you* make that dog?' her father asked. 'With your grandmother's scissors? Jolly good!'

Caroline practised and practised and after a week she could cut out anything she liked with the scissors. Even little houses, which she would cut out and then stick together. Everyone had heard about it and everyone in the neighbourhood came to look. There was the farm which sick little Caroline had made, with barns and stables and chickens and cows and pigs. And ducks, in a silver-paper pond.

'Good gracious, Caroline, how clever!'

One night Caroline had a strange dream. A tiny man, smaller than her little finger, skipped on to the table. 'You must make a palace,' he said.

'A palace?' asked Caroline. 'What for?'

'For the Queen,' said the little man. 'In three days' time she is giving a party and it's got to be in a beautiful new palace.'

'Made of paper?' asked Caroline.

'Naturally,' said the little man. 'And you must cut it out. With a big ballroom and two kitchens with stoves and a broad staircase to the upper rooms and turrets with flags and battlements and parapets and a double front door with a flight of steps. And you must make footmen too, and cooks and dancing girls. Lots of dancing girls, because it's going to be a big party.'

Caroline had to laugh about it next morning, and yet she could not forget her dream. 'You know,' she thought, 'I'm really going to make it. A whole palace. For my own pleasure.'

She began to snip and stick and stick and snip. Walls with windows in them, turrets with battlements, the ballroom floor, the steps leading upwards.

'What are you making, Caroline?' her mother asked.

'Oh, a palace.'

By evening she had stuck two walls together and part of the stairs.

That night she dreamed of the little man again. He tripped across the ballroom and gave the walls a push which made the paper crackle. 'Is it really sturdy enough?' he asked.

'Yes, of course,' said Caroline.

'And where are the kitchens?'

'I've still got to do them,' said Caroline.

She made the kitchens the next day and the upper rooms with the broad staircase leading up to them and the turrets with flags on them.

'You'll have to hurry up,' said the little man on the third night of her dream. 'You've only got one day left. What about the flight of steps? Where are the cooks and footmen and dancing girls? And one of the towers must be higher.'

Caroline began immediately after breakfast. She cut out twelve dancing girls and stuck them on one leg in a circle round the ballroom. She cut out seven cooks and stuck them on two legs by the stoves in the kitchens. She stuck an extra bit on the tower and made the steps and two big trees for the outside.

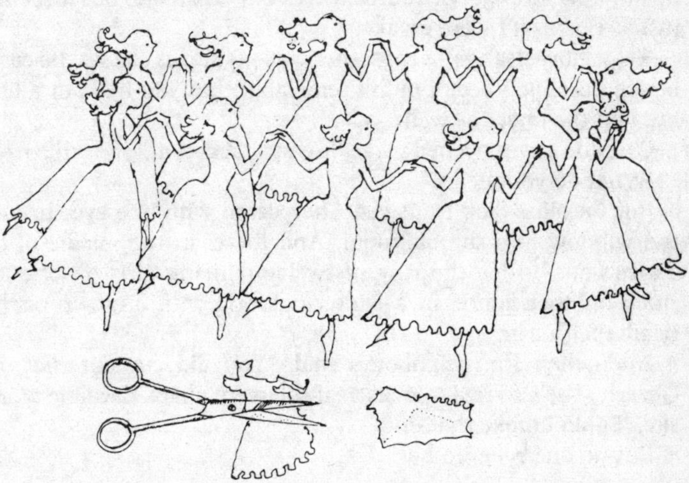

'Marvellous, child. Marvellous,' said her mother. 'Shall I put it away now?'

'On the table,' whispered Caroline.

But that night Caroline did not dream. No, she woke up instead. A light was shining in the room, a strange white light. She turned her head and then she saw it. In the middle of the table her paper palace stood sparkling and glittering as if a thousand lamps were burning inside it. Music was pouring from the windows and shadows were moving against the transparent paper walls – the shadows of people dancing.

'The party!' thought Caroline. She was longing to sit up, but her bad leg wouldn't let her.

Then the people in the palace started to sing and clap their hands and laugh and shout hooray and 'Long live the Queen!' and Caroline saw the shadows of skipping, swaying, leaping and whirling people dancing across the white walls.

Then she looked at the tall tower. There at the top stood the little man of her dream, on guard.

'Hello!' Caroline called to him.

At that moment everything fell dark and silent.

How strange, thought Caroline, and next morning she thought again: how strange. Of course it was only a dream, but it seemed just as real as if I were awake.

'I say, how strange,' her mother was saying, as she set the castle beside Caroline's bed. 'I didn't remember that you had put a little man on the tower as well.'

Caroline's eyes opened wide. 'It wasn't a dream,' she whispered.

'What do you mean?'

But Caroline didn't answer. She peered with one eye through the window into the ballroom. And there, in the middle of the dance floor, inside the ring of twelve dancing girls on one leg, stood another figure, in a wide cloak and with a crown on her head: the Queen.

And when the neighbours said, 'You did cut out *that* one cleverly, she's so real it looks as if she were alive,' Caroline would say, 'I didn't make that one.'

But no one believed her.

PAUL BIEGEL

THE FARM BROTHERS' BAND

There were once four brothers who lived with their sister, Betsy Ann, on a small farm just outside a little seaside village in Wales.

Now, nearly all the people who live in Wales are very fond of music. The four Jones brothers were real Welshmen. They were never happier than when they were making music. First, there was Davy-the-Drum with his *Rum-ti-tum-tum*! Then came Freddie-the-Flute with his *Tootle-too-toot*! The third brother was Triangle Tim with his *Ting-a-ling-ling*! The youngest brother was Trumpeter Tom with his *Too-too*! *Pom-pom*!

You can see they were almost like a band when they all played together. The only one who didn't join in was the brothers' sister, Betsy Ann. She said she was far too busy cooking and mending and cleaning – not to mention her hens and ducks – to make music with her brothers.

'The best I can do,' she would say, 'is to ring the dinner bell to fetch you all in before my good food gets spoiled.'

Of course, the brothers couldn't spend all their time playing their instruments. Davy-the-Drum was the porter at the small village station that only had a single-track line and four trains passing through it all day.

Freddie-the-Flute was the village postman, but, if there weren't too many letters to be delivered, he would pedal along the lanes gaily on his Post Office bicycle practising tunes on his flute.

Triangle Tim was the milkman and he took the milk from the farm cows all round the village each day.

Trumpeter Tom helped Betsy Ann with the farm work. He was a big strong cheery fellow and drove up and down the fields in his tractor or rounded up the sheep on the hillside with his old dog, as happy as could be.

One fine spring day when the blackthorn blossoms had sprinkled the hedges like snow and Triangle Tim found the first clump of pale primroses smiling up at him from a sheltered bank, Freddie-the-Flute came back to the farm full of excitement. But it wasn't until the brothers were all sitting round the big kitchen table enjoying Betsy Ann's steaming helpings of stew that he said anything to the rest of the family.

Then he put down his knife and fork, mopped up the last of the good rich gravy with a hunk of bread, and gave an important sort of cough.

'Well, brothers,' he said, as they looked at him in surprise, 'I've a bit of news for you all – good news, I fancy, and fun for our Betsy Ann, too.'

They all stopped eating and stared at Freddie-the-Flute who was generally a very quiet fellow.

'Mr Roberts-the-Bank was telling me this morning,' he went on, 'there's to be a Grand Carnival this summer and it's to be held in the field behind the station. People are coming from all the villages for miles around, and there's to be competitions and prizes and a fair and I don't know what. It'll be a real grand do, I can tell you.'

The brothers looked at Freddie-the-Flute in amazement and Betsy Ann gave a squeal of excitement. 'Well there's news, if you like!' she cried. 'Fancy Mr Roberts telling you all that, Freddie. We'll have to start saving up right away.'

Then they all began to chatter and laugh and ask questions till Freddie-the-Flute said, 'That is all I know yet, but there'll be posters and things so we can see what's on.'

'If there're musical competitions, I'm going in for a prize, that's for sure,' said big Trumpeter Tom.

'Me, too,' cried Davy-the-Drum.

'Why don't we make a band and do something all together?' suggested Triangle Tim.

Everyone thought that was a splendid idea.

How the brothers worked! They practised and practised till they knew their music so well they could have played it in their sleep!

At last the great day came. Betsy Ann had their Sunday suits and clean shirts all pressed and ready for them and she even found time to put a new ribbon in her straw hat. They *did* look smart as they set off for the village in their old car. It was quite a squash with their band things, too, but no one minded and they got to the field in plenty of time. And how everyone cheered and waved as the carnival procession marched along in the sunshine in all its finery. The four brothers walked together, playing away for all they were worth. Their faces grew as red as the rosebuds Betsy Ann had popped in their button-holes.

And then the judging began.

There were cheers for all the competitors, of course, but the biggest cheer of all seemed to be for Davy-the-Drum, with his *Rum-ti-tum-tum*, Freddie-the-Flute, with his *Tootle-too-toot*, Triangle Tim and his *Ting-a-ling-ling* and Trumpeter Tom and his *Too-too! Pom-pom!*

'It's the liveliest band I've heard for many a year,' said the judge. 'You have won first prize!' and he handed the brothers a shining silver cup and £2.50 in fifty-pence pieces!

'Well,' sighed Tom, who hadn't much spare breath left after all his blowing, 'that was a grand do, wasn't it?'

'Grand!' echoed his brothers and Betsy Ann.

'And this lovely silver cup!' cried Freddie.

'And all the money, too,' said Tim.

'I think we should have fifty pence each and give the other fifty pence to Betsy Ann who helped us so much,' said Trumpeter Tom.

'Good idea!' cried the other three as they went back through the farm gate to milk the cows, feed the chickens and ducks, and settle the farm for the night.

And can you guess how Betsy Ann spent her fifty pence? The very next time she went into market she spied a lovely little mouth organ in the toy shop window and she went right in and bought it! So, next time the brothers played their band, Betsy Ann had an instrument too. And, as she went round the house and farm doing her work, every now and then you could hear a faint little humming buzz. It was Betsy Ann practising on her mouth organ that she kept handily in the pocket of her apron!

URSULA HOURIHANE

GALLDORA AND THE MERMAID

One day Galldora was given a new dress and taken by Marybell to the seaside for a holiday.

'What a strange doll,' said the landlady, Mrs Cockle, when she saw Galldora.

'She's not really strange,' answered Marybell, 'she's just a rag doll.' Marybell spoke as stiffly as she could, because she was upset that the landlady was so rude about Galldora.

'Yes, my dear, I can see she is a rag doll,' said the landlady slowly, 'but she's strange all the same. She's very faded and flabby, poor thing, but perhaps the sea air will do her good. Let's hope so.'

'It's just her new dress that makes her look washed out,' explained Marybell, talking very fast to get in all she wanted to say; 'It is rather a bright colour. It's a piece of Mummy's worn-out dance dress. Mummy calls it flame colour. I'm not sure I like that colour myself. Blue's my favourite colour, that's why I bought a blue ribbon for Galldora's hair. I spent a whole four-pence on that ribbon. The colour's called king-fisher blue, and it doesn't look quite right with flame colour, but it is pretty all the same.'

'Very pretty,' Mrs Cockle said, adding, 'It's a pity about the safety-pin though, it's so large that it hides most of the ribbon.'

'Well, but, you see, Mrs Cockle, I had to pin it on Galldora's hair, because Galldora can't keep ribbons on her hair. It's wool hair, Mrs Cockle, and it's got a bit moth-eaten, and her head's such a funny shape too, sort of flattish, do you see what I mean?'

Galldora was held up for inspection. Mrs Cockle inspected Galldora's head. 'Yes, very flat, my dear, and a very odd shape.'

Now, Galldora was not at all pleased at this conversation. She loved being looked at, but she felt it was very rude indeed of people to make remarks about the shape of her head.

Human beings, she thought to herself, have no manners, no manners at all. Certainly none where dolls are concerned.

I think the discussion on Galldora's head would have spoilt the whole of Galldora's holiday if it hadn't been for an adventure that came her way on the first evening.

It was a wonderful adventure, and Galldora was able to tell all the other dolls and the teddy bears about it when she returned to the nursery. It happened like this. Marybell was so eager to rush down to the sands and the sea at once that her mother promised to take her down as soon as they had unpacked the spade, the bucket, and the swimsuits.

'We won't wait for lunch,' said Marybell's mother, 'we'll ask Mrs Cockle if she could make us some sandwiches and we'll eat them on the sands.'

Mrs Cockle understood all about little girls wanting to rush on to the sands and not waste a moment so she bustled about and produced a packed lunch.

'There you are, my dear,' she said to Marybell's mother, as she handed over the lunch, and turning to Marybell she added, 'That's right, love, you take that doll down and give her a good sea blow, that will do the poor thing a power of good.'

The sands and the sea were all that sands and sea should be.

The sands were silver white, stretching as far to the right and as far to the left as Marybell could see, and the great ocean was in a very gentle mood.

'Oh, Mummy,' said Marybell, 'I want to stay here always and always.'

'Well, we have till six o'clock,' answered Marybell's mother. 'Now, how about a paddle, Marybell, while I get the lunch set out? Then after lunch I'll help you build a sand castle, and later we will go and have a real swim.'

So after their lunch Marybell's mother helped Marybell to build the hugest and the most magnificent sand castle that Galldora had ever seen. It was so large that Marybell could stand in the middle courtyard without knocking any of the castle walls down. The castle had turrets and windows, and a moat, and a wall round the moat, with more turrets and more windows. When the castle was finished Galldora was sat on a sand-throne made especially for her. She sat there happily and proudly, staring out over the castle walls.

After a swim Marybell decided to look for shells. She and her mother were so happy collecting shells and shining wet pebbles

that Marybell's mother forgot all about the time. When she did look at her watch she was horrified.

'Quickly, Marybell,' she said, 'we mustn't be late the very first day. Mrs Cockle said she would have a high tea waiting for us at six, and it is six o'clock now.'

There was a lot of collecting up to be done. Wet towels and bathing-suits were crammed into one basket. Then into another basket went the paper wrappings of the lunch and the sun-hats and the sun-glasses, while in the bucket went the pebbles and shells. With all the pushing of this here and that there, both Marybell and Marybell's mother forgot Galldora. Marybell's mother did say, 'Have you got Galldora, Marybell?' and Marybell had answered, 'Yes, Mummy, I put her with my swim-suit.' And Marybell really thought she had. Galldora couldn't be seen, for the sand-throne she had been sitting on had collapsed, and she had sunk forward against the wall. She was still upright, and her head rested against a turret, but she was hidden and she couldn't see anything but sand. Galldora heard Marybell chattering as she and her mother hurried away from the beach, back to Mrs Cockle and high tea. Soon the beach grew very quiet except for the wild noises of sea-birds. Then the noise of the sea seemed to grow louder.

The half-hours went by, and the sky changed from blue to a flush of pink and yellow gold. If only Galldora could have seen how wonderful the sky was, for it looked as if some giant child of the sky-lands had tipped up a basket full of rose petals and set them floating down. Then the colour left the sky, and a silver bloom lingered on the sea and the sands. All the while the sound of the sea grew louder.

I know I'm not fancying it, said Galldora to herself. It's true, the sea is coming towards me inch by inch.

It was true. The tide was rolling in the white surf, and with the incoming tide a low wind had sprung up. The wind stirred the white sand and set the white horses riding far out at sea. It may have been the dragging of the sands, as the sea washed out before each incoming wave swept up, or it may have been the low wind shifting the sands, but whatever was the cause, the walls of the castle cracked and slowly, very slowly, crumbled.

'Gracious me,' gasped Galldora, 'I can see now – and how very different everything looks. Mrs Cockle wouldn't approve at all. Why, everything looks as pale and as washed-out as my face.'

The silver bloom about the scene turned clearer and harder. Shadows sprang like seaweed in a silver wash. All in the dark and the light of the waves were a million phosphorous sea life, that glowed so gaily it looked as if the fish were holding a great ball, far down below. The moon, like a full-sailed ship riding high, seemed to let drift a fishing-net of light to glitter and shimmer on the sea.

It's very beautiful, thought Galldora, but I rather wish I wasn't here. I think Mrs Cockle's boarding-house would be more cosy. Still, it's no good me wishing, as here I am and here I'll have to stay until Marybell finds me tomorrow.

All the time the sea crept closer, wave by wave. This began to worry Galldora.

I wish the sea would stop – just stop where it is, thought Galldora. If it doesn't my castle will soon be washed away and I with it. And then she sighed, 'Oh, dear, poor Marybell, she won't have a rag doll any more.'

Just then Galldora thought she heard sweet singing. I've got myself into such a state of nerves, I'm imagining all sorts of things, she told herself crossly. Why, that's only the noise of the sea or the wind or a bird. But try as Galldora would to make herself believe the singing noise was just natural noises, she couldn't. The singing grew louder and higher. I don't think I like that singing at all, thought Galldora, it makes me feel uncomfortable.

Then Galldora noticed a shape on one of the white horses far out in the sea. As the shape came nearer Galldora thought it was a girl. A girl with long, shining hair. And it was a girl. The girl was singing.

Nearer and nearer came the white horse and the girl with the long hair, until, with a sudden *splosh*, she was washed up on shore. Then Galldora saw she was not a proper girl, but a mermaid.

The mermaid was in a shocking temper. She clearly hated being on the shore. She stopped singing and lashed her tail, and was very thankful when the next wave lifted her up and washed her out into the sea again.

'Oh, do stop and talk to me, please!' called Galldora. 'I've never talked to a mermaid before. But perhaps you can't talk.'

'Of course I can, silly,' answered the mermaid. 'But where are you?'

'In here,' called Galldora. 'Here in the sand castle.' The mermaid swam closer to the shore to have a look.

'I can't see with all this hair,' said the mermaid at last, and she tossed her hair this way and that.

'I'm just near you,' explained Galldora, 'for the sea has come up to my castle walls, and I'm terribly afraid it will wash it and me away.'

The mermaid lifted up her silvery hair with her two hands. 'That's better,' she said. 'Ah, yes, I can see you now. My, aren't you small, and you haven't got much hair – how very strange.'

'Oh, yes, I know all about that,' said poor Galldora. 'And I've got a funny-shaped head, but I'm used to it, and it's *my* hair and *my* head, and, anyway, talking of hair, you've got far too much. You ought to have it cut off.'

'Cut it off – how do you do that?' asked the mermaid. Then Galldora realized at once she had made a very silly remark, because, of course, who would have scissors in the sea? 'Oh, I've changed my mind,' she said hurriedly, 'I shouldn't cut your hair off if I were you; it suits you.'

'If you had to choose between one eye and three eyes,' said the mermaid, 'which would you choose?'

'I've often had one eye,' said Galldora, 'and another one can always be sewn on, but three would look ugly, very ugly indeed. So I would choose one.'

'I'd choose three,' said the mermaid, 'a third one in the middle of my forehead, then when I opened my middle eye, the lashes would lift my hair a little, so I could see. It's a dreadful nuisance not being able to see properly. Look what happened just now. I got washed ashore, just because I couldn't see where I was going.'

'Yes, I do understand what you mean,' said Galldora thoughtfully.

'Can't you think of something to help me?' asked the mermaid.

'I'll try,' said Galldora. 'You can see now, though, can't you?'

'Yes, because I'm lifting my hair with my hands, but it gets trying.'

'Of course,' said Galldora. Then she asked, 'Do other mermaids have this trouble?'

'No,' answered the mermaid. 'It's because I'm a bad mermaid I have this trouble. The good mermaids sit on rocks and sing to the sailors, and it makes the sailors muddled and then they wreck their ships on the rocks. The ships sink, and the mermaids go swimming down and down into the wrecks and they find all sorts of treasures, like string and mirrors and combs. The mermaids make their hair behave by combing it, then they tie it up with the string, and then they look at themselves in the mirrors.'

'Just a moment,' said Galldora. 'I'm getting a bit muddled, or are you? Surely if mermaids wreck ships that's being very wicked and bad.'

'No, that's being good,' said the mermaid. 'Being bad is being like me, not wrecking ships, but just playing about in the sea. Oh, I love playing!'

'I think I'll have to think this out,' muttered Galldora, feeling very muddled.

Just then a crab who had been silently listening started to laugh and said, 'What a joke – thinking.'

'It's all very well for you to laugh,' said Galldora crossly, 'but you don't have to think this out like I do. You understand the sea and sea-creatures. I don't.'

'Don't try,' answered the crab. 'Some folks do things sideways, like me, some folks do things flat ways, like plaice, while other folks do things along, like eels do. But mermaids, they do things upside down.'

'Yes,' Galldora had a long think. 'That's very helpful,' she said. 'Thank you, Mr Crab, for telling me. I understand now. Being good is being bad to mermaids and being bad is being good, is that it?'

'It is and it isn't,' answered the crab, 'it just depends. Now, for wrecking their ships. You can't reason with mermaids, it's better to give them a "hello" in passing and let them be. Don't have no conversation with mermaids and above all don't listen to them singing. It will muddle you.'

'Thank you,' said Galldora, 'thank you very much, Mr Crab.'

'You're welcome,' mumbled the crab, as he walked away sideways.

'That was very kind of him,' said Galldora out loud.

'Oh, was it?' snapped the mermaid. 'I think it was most spiteful of that crab and he was just talking rubbish. Oh, do hurry up and think of something to keep the hair out of my eyes. My arms are aching, and I want to go and play!'

'I know,' said Galldora, 'I've got the very thing for you – my ribbon.'

'Give it to me,' said the mermaid, putting out a hand and letting half of her long hair fall down.

'Well, I can't exactly give it to you,' answered Galldora sadly, 'you will have to come and get it. I'm a doll, you see, and I can't walk.'

The mermaid swam about on the edge of the waves and peered at the rag doll, and got very cross. She pouted and flicked her tail and then said, 'I can't walk either, so we'll just have to wait for the sea to come up and wash you to me, that's all.'

'Oh, I do hope not, what will become of me then?' gasped Galldora.

'Don't you like the sea?' asked the mermaid in surprise.

'No.'

'That's funny, the sea is safe.'

'Yes, to you, because you are a mermaid, but I'm a rag doll, and rag dolls find the sea very unsafe, I can assure you.'

'What colour is your ribbon?' asked the mermaid, changing the subject.

'Blue,' said Galldora.

'I like blue,' said the mermaid.

'It's got a silver safety-pin holding the ribbon to my hair.'

'What's a safety-pin like? I can't see.'

'You've let your hair go all over your face again, that's why,' said Galldora.

'Well, my arms were aching so,' answered the mermaid. 'Oh, I do wish the sea would hurry up and wash you out!'

'Do you think it really will?' gasped Galldora in alarm.

'Oh, yes, of course,' answered the mermaid, 'I know it will. It's still coming in, and your castle wall is slowly crumbling.'

'If I am a good rag doll –' began Galldora, then she stopped. 'Of course,' she mumbled to herself, 'it's the other way round with mermaids.' So she started again. 'If I am a bad rag doll and let you have my ribbon for keeps and my safety-pin, will you be a bad mermaid in return and throw me out of the sea far behind the castle, where I will be safe?'

'Oh, yes, all right,' said the mermaid, 'let's be bad together,' which, of course, to the mermaid meant being good.

So when at last the sea broke through the castle walls and washed Galldora out the mermaid picked her up. The mermaid took her blue ribbon and the safety-pin, and then threw her over the crumbling castle on to the far dry sand.

'Thank you,' shouted Galldora, lying on her back in the sand-dunes. 'Does the ribbon work?' she called.

'Yes, rather,' shouted back the mermaid, 'I've tied some of my hair one side with the ribbon and pulled some of the other through the safety-pin. It's lovely. I can see now. I can go and play and play and play. I'll be able to play catch with the porpoises like I never did before, and grandmother's steps with the whales. What fun!'

Then, as the mermaid swam away singing, she turned just for a second and waved a last good-bye to the rag doll. Soon her song was lost in the song of the sea, and the silver flick of her silver tail was lost in the silver of the moon's light that spread upon the waters.

Galldora was found next day by Marybell, and Marybell knew at once that she must have had some strange adventure, for how else did the rag doll leave the sea-washed castle, and how did she lose her ribbon and the safety-pin?

'I hope it was a happy adventure,' said Marybell to Galldora. Galldora's shoe-button eyes shone back so brightly that Marybell knew it had indeed been a very happy adventure, and she was glad.

MODWENA SEDGWICK

THE PUDDING LIKE A NIGHT ON THE SEA

'I'm going to make something special for your mother,' my father said.

My mother was out shopping. My father was in the kitchen looking at the pots and the pans and the jars of this and that.

'What are you going to make?' I said.

'A pudding,' he said.

My father is a big man with wild black hair. When he laughs, the sun laughs in the window-panes. When he thinks, you can almost see his thoughts sitting on all the tables and chairs. When he is angry, me and my little brother Huey shiver to the bottom of our shoes.

'What kind of pudding will you make?' Huey said.

'A wonderful pudding,' my father said. 'It will taste like a whole raft of lemons. It will taste like a night on the sea.'

Then he took down a knife and sliced five lemons in half. He squeezed the first one. Juice squirted in my eye.

'Stand back!' he said, and squeezed again. The seeds flew out on the floor. 'Pick up those seeds, Huey!' he said.

Huey took the broom and swept them up.

My father cracked some eggs and put the yolks in a pan and the whites in a bowl. He rolled up his sleeves and pushed back his hair and beat up the yolks. 'Sugar, Julian!' he said, and I poured in the sugar.

He went on beating. Then he put in lemon juice and cream and set the pan on the stove. The pudding bubbled and he stirred it fast. Cream splashed on the stove.

'Wipe that up, Huey!' he said.

Huey did.

It was hot by the stove. My father loosened his collar and pushed at his sleeves. The stuff in the pan was getting thicker and thicker. He held the beater up high in the air. 'Just right!' he said, and sniffed in the smell of the pudding.

He whipped the egg whites and mixed them into the pudding. The pudding looked softer and lighter than air.

'Done!' he said. He washed all the pots, splashing water on the floor, and wiped the counter so fast his hair made circles around his head.

'Perfect!' he said. 'Now I'm going to take a nap. If something important happens, bother me. If nothing important happens, don't bother me. And – the pudding is for your mother. Leave the pudding alone!'

He went to the living room and was asleep in a minute, sitting straight up in his chair.

Huey and I guarded the pudding.

'Oh, it's a wonderful pudding,' Huey said.

'With waves on the top like the ocean,' I said.

'I wonder how it tastes,' Huey said.

'Leave the pudding alone,' I said.

'If I just put my finger in – there – I'll know how it tastes,' Huey said.

And he did it.

'You did it!' I said. 'How does it taste?'

'It tastes like a whole raft of lemons,' he said. 'It tastes like a night on the sea.'

'You've made a hole in the pudding!' I said. 'But since you did it, I'll have a taste.' And it tasted like a whole night of lemons. It tasted like floating at sea.

'It's such a big pudding,' Huey said. 'It can't hurt to have a little more.'

'Since you took more, I'll have more,' I said.

'That was a bigger lick than I took!' Huey said. 'I'm going to have more again.'

'Whoops!' I said.

'You put in your whole hand!' Huey said. 'Look at the pudding you spilled on the floor!'

'I am going to clean it up,' I said. And I took the rag from the sink.

'That's not really clean,' Huey said.

'It's the best I can do,' I said.

'Look at the pudding!' Huey said.

It looked like craters on the moon. 'We have to smooth this over,' I said. 'So it looks the way it did before! Let's get spoons.'

And we evened the top of the pudding with spoons, and while we evened it, we ate some more.

'There isn't much left,' I said.

'We were supposed to leave the pudding alone,' Huey said.

'We'd better get away from here,' I said. We ran into our bedroom and crawled under the bed. After a long time we heard my father's voice.

'Come into the kitchen, dear,' he said. 'I have something for you.'

'Why, what is it?' my mother said, out in the kitchen.

Under the bed, Huey and I pressed ourselves to the wall.

'Look,' said my father, out in the kitchen. 'A wonderful pudding.'

'Where is the pudding?' my mother said.

'WHERE ARE YOU BOYS?' my father said. His voice went through every crack and corner of the house.

We felt like two leaves in a storm.

'WHERE ARE YOU, I SAID!' My father's voice was booming.

Huey whispered to me, 'I'm scared.'

We heard my father walking slowly through the rooms.

'Huey!' he called. 'Julian!'

We could see his feet. He was coming into our room.

He lifted the bedspread. There was his face, and his eyes like black lightning. He grabbed us by the legs and pulled. 'STAND UP!' he said.

We stood.

'What do you have to tell me?' he said.

'We went outside,' Huey said, 'and when we came back, the pudding was gone!'

'Then why were you hiding under the bed?' my father said.

We didn't say anything. We looked at the floor.

'I can tell you one thing,' he said. 'There is going to be some beating here now! There is going to be some whipping!'

The curtains at the window were shaking. Huey was holding my hand.

'Go into the kitchen!' my father said. 'Right now!'

We went into the kitchen.

'Come here, Huey!' my father said.

Huey walked towards him, his hands behind his back.

'See these eggs?' my father said. He cracked them and put the yolks in a pan and set the pan on the counter. He stood a chair by the counter. 'Stand up here,' he said to Huey.

Huey stood on the chair by the counter.

'Now it's time for your beating!' my father said.

Huey started to cry. His tears fell in with the egg yolks.

'Take this!' my father said. My father handed him the egg beater. 'Now beat those eggs,' he said. 'I want this to be a good beating!'

'Oh!' Huey said. He stopped crying. And he beat the egg yolks.

'Now you, Julian, stand here!' my father said.

I stood on a chair by the table.

'I hope you're ready for your whipping!'

I didn't answer. I was afraid to say yes or no.

'Here!' he said, and he set the egg whites in front of me. 'I want these whipped and whipped well!'

'Yes, sir!' I said, and started whipping.

My father watched us. My mother came into the kitchen and watched us.

After a while Huey said, 'This is hard work.'

'That's too bad,' my father said. 'Your beating's not done!' And he added sugar and cream and lemon juice to Huey's pan and put the pan on the stove. And Huey went on beating.

'My arm hurts from whipping,' I said.

'That's too bad,' my father said. 'Your whipping's not done.'

So I whipped and whipped, and Huey beat and beat.

'Hold that beater in the air, Huey!' my father said.

Huey held it in the air.

'See!' my father said. 'A good pudding stays on the beater. It's thick enough now. Your beating's done.' Then he turned to me. 'Let's see those egg whites, Julian!' he said. They were puffed up and fluffy. 'Congratulations, Julian!' he said. 'Your whipping's done.'

He mixed the egg whites into the pudding himself. Then he passed the pudding to my mother.

'A wonderful pudding,' she said. 'Would you like some, boys?'

'No, thank you,' we said.

She picked up a spoon. 'Why, this tastes like a whole raft of lemons,' she said. 'This tastes like a night on the sea.'

ANN CAMERON

Green Grobblop

At first nobody knew what the green grobblop was or even where it came from. Ben found it on the doorstep one Monday morning. He came running in from the garden calling to his mother.

'Come and see! There's a funny green hairy thing out here. It's ever so small and ever so sad. Can I play with it?'

Ben's Mum, who was in the kitchen doing the washing, came to have a look.

'I don't know what it is,' she said, 'and it doesn't look very clean. I think I'd better give it a good wash before you play with it.'

She always washed everything on a Monday. So she washed it. She was going to peg it up to dry when she heard it say, 'Don't peg me up on the clothes line. A green grobblop like me should be put in a nice warm room.'

Ben's Mum was so surprised to hear the grobblop speak, she said, 'Oh, I'm sorry!' and asked, 'What did you say your name was?'

'I'm a green grobblop,' it said, and it did look so small and sad. Ben's Mum was a kind lady. She took it at once and put it on the curly cuddly rug in the sitting-room.

'That's much better,' said the grobblop, nodding its small green head. 'Now I should like tea and chocolate biscuits and some bananas.'

'There is only one banana,' said Ben, who was looking forward to eating it for his tea.

'Well, that will have to do for now then,' sighed the grobblop, looking smaller and sadder than ever. 'But in future, I would like three for my tea.'

After he had eaten the banana, the grobblop had four helpings of biscuits. He was just drinking his fifth cup of tea when Ben's Dad came home from work.

'What's that?' asked Ben's Dad. When Ben and his Mum told him, Ben's Dad had to agree that the grobblop did look small and sad.

'And it will need to be well looked after,' he said.

All the rest of the week the grobblop sat on the curly cuddly rug. Ben's Mum fed him and Ben played with him whenever he wanted. At the end of the week Ben's Mum said: 'I'm afraid I shall need some more money now that we have a grobblop to feed. It does eat rather a lot.'

'I can see that,' said Ben's Dad, and he looked worried. He wasn't at all sure that his boss would pay him more money just because he now had a green grobblop to feed.

'Perhaps,' he said, 'when the green grobblop gets bigger and stronger, he'll be able to do some useful jobs about the house.'

'I hope so,' agreed Ben's Mum. She had been doing everything for the grobblop, giving him the biggest helpings, letting him have the most comfortable place to sit in the sitting-room and the warmest blankets on his bed.

'I can think of lots of useful things he could do,' said Ben's Mum.

No sooner was this said than the grobblop said, 'I'll have to go to bed. I'm not at all well.'

The doctor was called and he came almost at once. He wasn't used to treating grobblops, but he said, 'He does look green and small and sad! He needs someone to look after him. He's to stay in bed a day or two and take this medicine to make him well and strong.'

The grobblop liked his medicine almost as much as he liked tea and biscuits and bananas. He liked staying in bed even better than he liked lying on the curly cuddly rug in the sitting-room. So he stayed in bed and had all his meals brought up. All the time he was growing bigger and stronger, Ben's Mum grew thinner and more tired, until one day, she said, 'I'm quite worn out.' Ben's Dad sent her to bed and called the doctor who said, 'You're to stay in bed a day or two and let someone look after you.'

The grobblop heard what the doctor said. He peeped in to see Ben's Mum. 'She does look so sad and small,' thought the grobblop who was now big and strong. He felt ashamed. He went downstairs at once.

He cleaned the kitchen, dusted the rooms, and made a delicious meal which he took up to her on a tray. He did this every day until Ben's Mum was well again. Then he said to her, 'I've come to say it's time I went away.'

'You don't have to go,' said Ben's Mum. 'You really can stay as long as you like.'

But the grobblop replied, 'No, I'm big enough and strong enough to look after myself now. I won't forget how well you looked after me and I'll write to you sometimes.'

Ben and his Mum and Dad were quite sorry to say goodbye to the grobblop. He went to live at the seaside and he did write to them. He sent them some lovely picture postcards and he's asked them all to come and stay with him for their next summer holiday.

EUGENIE SUMMERFIELD

MISS HICKORY

Miss Hickory heard heavy footsteps, clump, clumping along the stones of the pasture, then approaching her lilac bush. Out of the corner of one sharp little black eye she could see a pair of large yellow feet but she did not turn her head. As a matter of fact Miss Hickory had difficulty in turning her head. It was a hickory nut that had grown with an especially sharp and pointed nose. Her eyes and mouth were inked on. Her body was an apple-wood twig formed like a body with two arms and two legs, hands and feet, as twigs sometimes grow. To this body Miss Hickory's nut head was glued. She wore a blue-and-white checked gingham dress. A white cap with ruffles was tied in a smart bow beneath her chin. Many persons, looking first at Miss Hickory, would have said that she was a country doll, made by Miss Keturah who kept the notions store in Hillsborough, and given to Ann. But not you or I. The tilt of her sharp little nose, her pursed mouth and her keen eyes were not those of a doll. You and I would have known Miss Hickory as the real person that she was.

A black shadow passed the doorsill of Miss Hickory's house. A coarse *caw* seemed intended to catch her attention, but she continued sweeping with her broom that was made of pine needles. She had just finished her tea and her acorn cup and saucer, neatly washed, stood on a shelf above the stove. A bed of discarded pullets' feathers covered with a bright quilt of patched sumac leaves was ready for pleasant dreams. Miss Hickory's house was made of corncobs, notched, neatly fitted together and glued. It stood beneath the lilac bush that was so sweet and purple when in bloom, so thickly green and cheerful with birds all summer long. If one had to live in town, Miss Hickory had always said, take a house under a lilac bush.

Soon, through her front door, the sunset would toss a few coloured pieces from the orchard sky. Soon, too, the sun would drop like the biggest apple in the world, red and round, behind Temple Mountain that guarded the orchard spring, summer, autumn and winter, world without end. The sun set earlier now, for it was late September. Miss Hickory swept more briskly to warm herself. Thinking of cold weather made her shiver. But a large dark head with beady eyes and a long bill, thrust in through the window, stopped her.

'Are you at home, Miss Hickory?' Crow asked in his hoarse voice.

'Well, what do you think, if you ever do think?' she asked. 'I heard your big yellow clodhoppers, and I saw you pass by. If you think there is one kernel of corn left in my house walls that you can peck out you are mistaken. You have eaten them all.'

'Dear lady!' said Crow, stopping, entering and making himself at home. 'Always so polite, so generous!'

A small smile seemed to move the wrinkles of Miss Hickory's face. 'Here.' She took from her pocket a few hard yellow kernels and held them out. Crow gobbled, choked, bowed low.

'Don't try to thank me,' she urged. 'You'll get the hiccups. What is the news? If there is any, you have heard it.'

'Precisely why I am here, as they put it over the radio,' he said. 'News indeed, and it concerns you.'

Miss Hickory sat down on her toadstool, spreading her skirts neatly to cover her ankles. Crow rested his wings comfortably, eased his toes and leaned against the wall. These two might spit and tiff, but they had fellow feelings. Crow made no pretensions; he was a country man. The earth owed him a living and so he helped himself to cherries and corn. Summer boarders, the bluebirds, thrushes, and larks, could fend for themselves, Crow felt, paying high prices for any berries and seeds that they got from his feeding ground. But he knew what was going on throughout the entire countryside. He was tough and weatherwise. He set the date for Old Crow Week in Hillsborough every spring, and so started the season with noisy promise. He could walk as well as fly, which meant that he got around more than most birds. He knew that Miss Hickory had once been part of a tree and he respected her for that ancestry. In certain ways they were alike. He waited for her to speak.

'Well,' she said at last.

Crow folded his wings over his stomach and pointed his beak at Miss Hickory.

'Great-granny Brown is closing this house for the winter. She plans to live in the Women's City Club on Beacon Hill, Boston, until spring.' The house was full of stillness for a while, thick with thoughts that could not break it. His words stunned Miss Hickory. She could not speak.

'I know,' Crow said at last, 'that you expected to live another winter, house and all, on Great-granny Brown's kitchen window-sill. You expected Ann to drop in almost every day and bring you something useful, a little iron stove, a pot or a tin tea-kettle. But the entire family is going to Boston. Ann is to be put into school there.' Crow rolled his eyes towards the ceiling, pretending to be shocked. Truly, however, he was enjoying himself. A love of gossip is hatched from every crow's egg.

Miss Hickory arose. She came close to him, her sharp little nose almost touching his face.

'They could not! They would not!'

'Ah, yes, Miss Hickory,' he assured her. 'Two-leggers who have been to Boston long for wings. Only we country people who can fly never feel the need of a city. Now, I once knew a starling who went to the Public Gardens in Boston for a visit, but –'

'Stop! Don't gabble.' Miss Hickory twisted her hands in distress. 'Come to the point.'

'The point is yours, dear lady.' Crow tapped her shoulder playfully with one wing-tip. 'You have seen through Great-granny Brown's kitchen window how deep the snowdrifts are in New Hampshire. I'll wager that there were days when you could not see through the windows. The winters are long and hard here, Miss Hickory.'

'What could one do?' she begged. She would not believe him yet.

'Don't feel too badly, as if they had forgotten you,' he said kindly, 'Ann has other matters than dolls to fill her mind now. Great-granny Brown was born and bred in New Hampshire. She expects you to be equal to any weather. You'll have to move, Miss Hickory.'

'Where?' She went over to the window and looked west. There each year the forest, wild and deep, marched closer to the Old Place. They had both forgotten to admire the sunset. The afterglow, like a blanket of woven rainbows, had folded about Temple Mountain.

'Aye, that's the rub!' Crow replied hoarsely.

Miss Hickory stamped her foot.'Don't talk like a Poll-Parrot. Whatever you hear, either the radio or William Shakespeare, you repeat. You know you can't read a word.'

Crow bowed his head humbly. 'Right you are, but what I meant was that we shall have to make a plan, and make it speedily. You can't live under a lilac bush all winter.'

'We? This isn't your home. It belongs to me. I like it here, I can't move. Where would I take my stove, my pot and my tea-kettle, my cup and saucer and my bed? If I lived in a crow's nest, with no nice house furnishings and no good housekeeping...' She could not say any more. She could only look with love and fear at her four corncob walls.

'You give me an idea, Miss Hickory.' Crow balanced himself on one foot and scratched his head with the other.

'I will have no idea of yours.'

'But a little change is good for us all,' Crow said, smirking. 'You must remember, dear lady, that you weren't born with a cup and saucer in your hand.'

It was more than Miss Hickory could stand. She lost her temper. 'I believe that this is all a piece of gossip on your part, Crow. I shall never believe that the Old Place is empty until I ask Mr T. Willard-Brown. He will tell me the truth. As for you, Crow –' She stood as tall and brave as she could beside her door. 'Get out of my house!' she ordered.

'As you wish.' Crow walked in a dignified manner towards the door. 'But don't worry. Something is bound to turn up!'

'I won't move!' she repeated as he stepped across the threshold. But he tapped her head lightly with his beak.

'Hardheaded, that's what you are!' And with that Crow walked off in the direction of the pine wood, he and the falling night one, in the colour of dusk.

Miss Hickory put her twig hands up to her nut head. Crow, she knew, was right. Her head was undoubtedly hard. She moved slowly about her house, lifting a stove lid to poke the red coals, turning down her bedspread. But as she comforted herself with these homely tasks, a feeling that she had never experienced before came to Miss Hickory. Perhaps it was caused by the sap that was still in her twig body. Perhaps it was the essence of the sweet nut inside the hard shell of her head. Whatever caused it, Miss Hickory began to cry. Tears came out of her eyes and rolled down her wrinkled cheeks. They fell so fast that she had to staunch them with her cap ties. It was dark then, so no one saw her break down. No one heard Miss Hickory sob, 'It isn't true! I won't move! Mr T. Willard-Brown will tell me tomorrow that I only had a bad dream.'

'A good day to finish my canning,' Miss Hickory said to herself as she built up a wood fire and started towards the forest for berries.

It was a beautiful day, crisp but with warm sunshine that made her forget Crow's warning visit. Crow was so ready with raucous chit-chatter that she did not take him seriously. 'He always has something to say and likes to hear himself say it,' she reminded herself as she put a small rush basket over her arm and stepped briskly off on her twig feet. Although the torches that the goldenrod had lighted along the October road towered above Miss Hickory's head, she found her way easily in and out among them. Their brightness made her feel gay. Farther on the purple asters made a royal canopy beneath which she walked proudly until she came to the edge of the woods. She left the road and was at once in the deep green of the pines.

Miss Hickory's nose was as keen as a fox's. The smell of pine trees never failed to go to her head. She could not explain why, but when she was alone in the woods, sniffing rich earth, wandering through the lacy lanes of ferns, and smelling the pines, she felt like another person. She wished that she had time to dig up one of the tiny new hemlock trees to set out at the front of her corncob house, an idea that she had treasured for some time. But the cold of the woods, now that she had left the sunny road, made her realize that there would not be many more berrying days. She knelt down, dug away the leaves that already were making a thick covering on the earth.

It always surprised her to feel how warm the earth kept under the leaves, even on a cold day. She dug them aside, here and there, uncovering the vines that she wanted. It was as delightful to thrust her twig arms up to the elbows in the warm tangle as to sniff the woods. She began to pick the bright red berries and fill her basket. There was no time to lose, she knew. Cock-Pheasant lived close by and was a famous berry-picker.

Checkerberries first! They stood up straight, in plain sight on their stems, and could be picked fast. But for preserving and storing away in her acorn jugs for the winter, Miss Hickory knew that checkerberry preserve needed a good deal of sweetening, more honey than she had been able to save that season. She picked up a few checkerberry leaves. They were tasty and crisp served with a cup of tea.

Next, the partridgeberries that ripened close to the ground, little crimson balls in twins, two growing side by side secretly on their low-lying running vine. Miss Hickory canned partridgeberries whole in their own sweet juice. As she finished gathering berries and started home with her filled basket she remembered something that Cock-Pheasant had once told her.

'When the partridgeberries are ripe,' Cock-Pheasant had said, 'it is only two full moons before the first snowfall.'

When she came home, Miss Hickory saw that the entire front of her house was covered by the fat brindled haunches of Mr T. Willard-Brown. He was enjoying the sunshine that trickled down through the bare lilac bushes and waving his long tail to and fro like a banner. He was a wandering barn cat, a hunter of renown, but Miss Hickory liked him. Mr T. Willard-Brown lived a secret life closer to the ground than did Crow. He was a newsy man and willing to share his stories.

'You are late this morning,' she told him.

'The milking was late,' he explained. 'I can't start the day without my regular breakfast of a dish of warm milk, right from the cow.'

Miss Hickory set down her basket of berries, came close, and looked sharply into Mr T. Willard-Brown's green eyes.

'That would have been a better story, my friend,' she said, 'if you had washed your face before you told it. There is a feather sticking out of your mouth.' She flipped it off.

'Oh, my ears and whiskers,' he explained in mock chagrin. 'However did I get into feathers so early in the morning? Now, if it had been teatime here at the Old Place and I had dropped in and someone had urged me to take a nap on one of those soft feather pillows –' He purred loudly to cover his embarrassment.

'Never mind,' she said. 'We all know your habits, Mr T., and I am glad to see you this morning. Crow called yesterday.

'Don't speak of him!' Mr T. Willard-Brown spat. 'I wouldn't eat crow on a wager. The last time I saw Crow he walked right towards me and said a bad word. I spat at him.'

'If you ate crow occasionally you might be a better man,' she told him. 'What I was about to say when you interrupted me was that Crow spoke of the family as planning to leave Hillsborough for the winter. He said that Great-granny Brown was thinking of living at the Women's City Club on Beacon Hill, Boston, and Ann was going to school there. Nothing but hearsay on his part, of course.'

Mr T. Willard-Brown arose, stretched and yawned. 'Not a plan, not hearsay, my love,' he told Miss Hickory, 'but the truth. They have gone!'

She listened without words, her eyes full of terror. He continued:

'You ought to get about more, Miss Hickory. All summer you have stayed here under the lilacs, only going to the woods for berries, or on Sunday when Jack-in-the-Pulpit preached. If you had gone around to the front of the house lately you would have seen trunks coming down from the attic.'

'Gone!' she breathed at last. Now she knew that it was true. She would not let him see her cry. Instead she stamped her twig feet.

'It's all your fault, Mr T. They had to leave to get away from *you*, scratching on doors and purring in the kitchen for milk. You are only a cat with a cat's ways. I shall tell all Hillsborough what your given name is. *Tippy*, because you have a white tip to your tail. Willard is for the barn where you were born. Brown is pretence. The hyphen is putting on airs. You are sly, Tippy. I always suspected it.'

He purred loudly, curling his claws and smiling. 'I am so famous a mouser that my given name and my humble birth are always overlooked. If you doubt Crow and me, why not go around to the front of the house and look in? See for yourself.' He walked, with flowing tail, towards the barn.

Miss Hickory was unable to move for a space. She watched Mr T. Willard-Brown, swinging his sides and disappearing at last through the wide red doors of the barn. Then she walked slowly away from the lilac bush, the corncob house, her basket of berries. She skirted the garden, crossed the lawn and came to the pink rambler-rose trellis beside the front porch. Up the trellis she climbed, braving the sharp thorns, up, up, until she could peer underneath the crack of the window where the shade was not completely pulled down.

Blue Rocking Chair stood empty and still. The fireplace was boarded. The family bible on the centre table was folded carefully in a white towel. The shining brass pendulum of the grandfather cluck hung motionless and the hands pointed to eight o'clock. It must, by the shadow on the lawn sundial, be noon now. The Old Farmer's Almanac that had hung by a loop of string on the wall was gone. She had been alone, without knowing it, for some time.

She knew now that everything that Crow and Mr T. Willard-Brown had told her was true. Her head would have whirled if it could. She felt too weak to hold on to the rose trellis, but she backed slowly down. Mr T. Willard-Brown was waiting for her, having come softly around the corner of the house.

'Well, there you are, Miss Hickory,' he purred. 'Two of us in the same fix. Why not come over to the barn with me? It is to be kept open all winter and I have been offered a permanent position as head ratter.'

'I wasn't born to live in a barn,' she told him desperately.

'Where then?' he asked.

'I am going home,' she said. 'Today I shall finish my canning.'

'Home?' He smiled. 'Amusing, that! I just passed your house and it was occupied. You know Chipmunk of course, who lives in the stone wall and has been so spoiled with gifts of peanuts that he expects to be supported? He has moved into your house, Miss Hickory. I should say that he is there for the winter. He was finishing his dinner when I saw him, your basket of berries.'

Miss Hickory never remembered how long she sat on the ground under the rambler-rose trellis. If she had been living in her own home at the back of the house she might have cried, but that small corncob home, so cosy and familiar, was now occupied by Chipmunk. Here, with the open road in front, she was too proud to show her sorrow. More than sorrow, she felt despair. She became damp with the heavy dew and then stiff with the first frost. The wind whistling down from Temple Mountain whipped her wet skirts around her shivering legs. None of the few passers-by noticed her. Mr T. Willard-Brown, warm and busy in the barn, gave her no thought. A light flurry of snow powdered her cap.

But one day, when Miss Hickory was sure that her end was near, down the road from the orchard, walking briskly, came Crow. Would he, too, pass her by? No, Crow turned into the front path and approached. He came close to the spot where Miss Hickory huddled under the poor shelter of the rambler-rose trellis. He raised one foot in salute.

'Dear lady!' Crow croaked, ignoring her bedraggled state. He understood that she had suffered a great loss. He was a busybody and had heard about Chipmunk.

'Don't try to explain, Miss Hickory,' he said hoarsely. 'We all have our troubles. I told you that something would turn up. It has.'

'What?' She stood up and leaned against the trellis.

'First of all,' he told her, 'you must realize that a change, travel, a new scene, are good for all of us. You especially, Miss Hickory, need a change. You have been living for two years with those who feel that they need a grocery store, a Ford car, a stove, and storm windows. You have grown soft.'

She held out her arms, no longer proud.

'Don't preach to me, Crow! What has turned up?'

'A new home for you.' He gave a hop-jig step and a swing for show. 'Don't ask any questions, but come along with me. There isn't any time to lose. I shall very likely be off for good tomorrow and I want to see you well settled-in before I leave. Come with me, dear lady.'

Miss Hickory stumbled weakly towards Crow, but he caught her underneath one wide black wing. His wing was like a tent, warm and strong. His big yellow feet guided her small twig ones and the two left the Old Place behind and took to the road. He shortened his steps to suit hers, talking earnestly in his rough voice as he led her towards the orchard.

'You spoke of the untidiness of my nest. How right you are, Miss Hickory. Sticks, chaff and bark are all I ever use. But please realize that I am a man of affairs. I spend my days here and there, in the cornfield, the orchard, the vegetable garden. All I need in the way of a home is a place to hang my hat. But my nest is built high at the top of a tall pine tree as a lookout. From it I saw your new home.'

They reached the orchard.

'Turn this way,' he told her. 'We are going to follow McIntosh Lane along the hillside. You can't imagine how sheltered it is there, under the lee of the mountain with the pine woods up above for a windbreak. Lean on me, Miss Hickory. We are almost there.'

As they found and took the stubble-grown path where the older apple trees had twisted in odd bent shapes, the better to climb the hillside of the orchard and reach the sun, Miss Hickory felt herself floating, rather than trudging along. She was lifted off her feet every now and then as she clung to Crow's wing. She felt again the energy that the woods always gave her. The exercise of trying to keep up with Crow warmed her. Her heart pounded with excitement, for she believed that Crow was helping her to begin a great adventure. Perhaps a small log cabin with a fireplace and a chimney was waiting on beyond. When she had signed the lease she would return, evict Chipmunk and move her things up there to the hillside on McIntosh Lane.

'Is it much farther?' she gasped.

Crow was muttering and did not answer at once. He had never been able to count above one. One cherry, gulp it down. One plump green pea. One mouthful of corn. His father had taught him the corn-planting Rule.

One for the cut-worm
One for the crow,
One for the farmer . . .

'Never mind the rest of it,' Crow's father had said. 'It signifies nothing for us until later: "Two to grow".'

So Crow was not counting the trees on the hillside, but naming them.

'Cherry. Northern Spy. Clapp's Favourite Pear. McIntosh. McIntosh. Mc – Mc – Tosh – Tosh.' His tongue was becoming twisted. 'Here we are!' he told her at last as they were halfway or so along the hillside and deep among the leafless gnarled shapes of the apple trees. He stopped beneath one that had not seemed worth pruning that spring. The branches touched the ground and it leaned comfortably towards the slope of the hill, away from the wind. He loosed his hold on Miss Hickory and hopped towards a low-lying bough. 'Climb up!' he ordered.

'But – I don't understand.' She hesitated.

Crow spread his wings and disappeared among the branches of the apple tree but his voice croaked down to her:

'He who hesitates is lost. Do you or do you not want to live until spring? Climb, I told you!'

She grasped the low bough. How homelike it felt in her strong little twig fingers!

'Swing a bit and then jump!' Crow's call came to her from higher up. This, she decided, was a game that he wanted her to learn. She pulled on the bough, swayed pleasantly a moment and then jumped to another branch farther on.

'Keep on!' Crow croaked. 'Climb along up.'

So she continued to swing, jump and climb, feeling more adventurous and bold with each step. Up, up, Miss Hickory climbed into the apple tree until the ground was dizzying to look down upon and she could see Temple Mountain, keeping vigil to the west.

'How much farther?' she called.

'Here you are,' he answered from a perch right beside her. 'Carefully now. Easy does it. How's this, dear lady, for your new home?'

She looked in astonishment at what he pointed out to her: a large and deep nest resting securely in a crotch of the apple tree. Crow knew that it might not suit her at first sight so he began to argue and boast, like a real estate agent.

'Light and heat free, whenever the sun shines. A long lease. Although Robin built it for his own use and planned to stay north this winter, Mr T. Willard-Brown drove him away. Hooks for hanging your clothes; Robin builds carelessly and leaves twigs sticking out. Insulated against the cold with good country mud.' Crow's sales talk went on and on, but Miss Hickory had not listened after he had mentioned Mr T. Willard-Brown. No cat, she decided, would drive *her* out of her home. She balanced on a bough and inspected the empty nest. It was indeed well placed, sheltered and strong. As she peered inside she saw that the wind had cushioned the empty nest deeply with milkweed down and lined it with rose-brown oak leaves. She stepped inside and sank down deliciously into its warm comfort.

'Not bad at all, Crow,' she admitted.

'It struck me favourably,' he croaked.

The nest was so well suited to her size that when she stood up, she had to stretch a bit to pull herself out. When she lay down, as she now did, for she was very tired, she was snug and unseen. She was alone in a world that had no need of the things she had left behind.

'I don't know what I shall do here all winter,' she said, 'without a broom in my hands.'

'You'll find plenty to do,' he told her. 'New things to collect, new friends, new places to explore. Well, it's time I was off.'

'I am greatly obliged to you, Crow.' She leaned over the edge of the nest as Crow opened his wings.

'Don't give it a thought,' he said.

'How long until spring?' she ventured to ask. 'They took the Old Farmer's Almanac to Boston.'

'It doesn't matter,' he assured her. 'Spring always comes. Remember this, though, dear lady. This is important. Get it through your head. *Keep your sap running!*'

Crow spread his wings, cawed loudly and started. Miss Hickory watched Crow cross the Old Place, the barn, the woods, then disappear as he flew towards the south.

CAROLYN SHERWIN BAILEY

FATHER CHRISTMAS

One day Polly was in the kitchen, washing currants and sultanas to put in a birthday cake, when the front-door bell rang.

'Oh dear,' said Polly's mother, 'my hands are all floury. Be

a kind girl, Polly, and go and open the door for me, will you?'

Polly was a kind girl, and she dried her hands and went to the front door. As she left the kitchen, her mother called after her.

'But don't open the door if it's a wolf!'

This reminded Polly of some of her earlier adventures, and before she opened the door, she said cautiously, through the letter box, 'Who are you?'

'A friend,' said a familiar voice.

'Which one?' Polly asked. 'Mary?'

'No, not Mary.'

'Jennifer?'

'No, not Jennifer.'

'Penelope?'

'No. At least I don't think so. No,' said the wolf decidedly, 'not Penelope.'

'Well, I don't know who you are then,' Polly said. 'I can't guess. You tell me.'

'Father Christmas.'

'Father Christmas?' said Polly. She was so much surprised that she nearly opened the front door by mistake.

'Father Christmas,' said the person on the doorstep. 'With a sack full of toys. Now be a good little girl, Polly, and open the door and I'll give you a present out of my sack.'

Polly didn't answer at once.

'Did you say Father Christmas?' she asked at last.

'Yes, of course I did,' said the wolf loudly. 'Surely you've heard of Father Christmas before, haven't you? Comes to good children and gives them presents and all that. But not, of course, to naughty little girls who don't open doors when they're told to.'

'Yes,' Polly said.

'Well, then, what's wrong with that? You know all about Father Christmas and I'm pretending to be – I mean, here he is. I don't see what's bothering you and making you so slow.'

'I've heard of Father Christmas, of course,' Polly agreed. 'But not in the middle of the summer.'

'Middle of the what?' the wolf shouted through the door.

'Middle of the summer.'

There was a short silence.

'How do you know it's the summer?' the wolf asked argumentatively.

'We're making Mother's birthday cake.'

'Well? I don't see what that has to do with it.'

'Mother's birthday is in July.'

'Perhaps she's rather late in making her cake?' the wolf suggested.

'No, she isn't. She's a few days early, as a matter of fact.'

'You mean it's going to be her birthday in a day or two?'

'You've got it, Wolf,' Polly agreed.

'So we're in July now?'

'Yes.'

'It's not Christmas?'

'No.'

'Not even if we happened to be in Australia? They have Christmas in the summer there, you know,' the wolf said persuasively.

'But not here. It's nearly half a year till Christmas,' Polly said firmly.

'A pity,' the wolf said, 'I really thought I'd got you that time. I must have muddled up my calendar again - it's so confusing, all the weeks starting with Mondays.'

Polly heard the would-be Father Christmas clumping down the path from the front door; she went back to the currants.

The weeks went by; Mother's birthday was over and forgotten, holidays by the sea marked the end of summer and the beginning of autumn, and it was not until the end of September, when the leaves were turning yellow and brown, and the days were getting shorter and colder, that Polly heard from the wolf again. She was in the sitting-room when the telephone bell rang; Polly lifted the receiver.

'I ont oo thpeak oo Folly,' a very muffled voice said.

'I'm sorry,' Polly said, politely, 'I really can't hear.'

'Thpeak oo Folly.'

'I still can't quite hear,' Polly said.

'I ont oo – oh BOTHER these beastly whiskers,' said quite a different voice. 'There, now can you hear? I've taken bits of them off.'

'Yes, I can hear all right,' Polly said puzzled. 'But how can you take off your whiskers?'

'They weren't really mine. I mean they're mine, of course, but not in the usual way. I didn't grow them, I bought them.'

'Well,' Polly asked, 'how did you keep them on before you took them off?'

'Stuck them on with gum,' the voice replied cheerfully. 'But I haven't taken that bit off yet. The bit I took off was the bit that goes all round your mouth. You know, a moustache. It got awfully in the way of talking, though. The hair kept on getting into my mouth.'

'It sounded rather funny,' Polly agreed. 'But why did you have to put it on?'

'So as to look like the real one.'

'The real what?'

'Father Christmas, of course, silly. How would I be able to make you think I was Father Christmas if I didn't wear a white beard and all that cotton woolly sort of stuff round my face, and a red coat and hood and all that?'

'Wolf,' said Polly solemnly – for of course it couldn't be anyone else – 'do you mean to say you were pretending to be Father Christmas?'

'Yes.'

'And then what?'

'I was going to say if you'd meet me at some lonely spot – say the crossroads at midnight – I'd give you a present out of my sack.'

'And you thought I'd come?'

'Well,' said the wolf persuasively, 'after all I look exactly like Santa Claus now.'

'Yes, but I can't see you.'

'Can't See Me?' said the wolf, in surprise.

'We can't either of us see each other. You try, Wolf.'

There was a long silence. Polly rattled the receiver.

'Wolf!' she called. 'Wolf, are you there?'

'Yes,' said the wolf's voice, at last.

'What are you doing?'

'Well, I was having a look. I tried with a small telescope I happened to have by me, but I must admit I can't see much. The trouble is that it's so terribly dark in there. Hold on for a minute. Polly, I'm just going to fetch a candle.'

Polly held on. Presently, she heard a fizz and a splutter as the match was struck to light the candle. There was a long pause, broken by the wolf's heavy breathing. Polly heard him muttering: 'Not down there . . . Try the other end then . . . Perhaps if I unscrew this bit . . . Let's see this bit of wire properly . . .'

There was a deafening explosion, which made poor Polly jump. Her ear felt as if it would never hear properly again. Obviously the wolf had held his candle too near to the wires and something had exploded.

'I do hope he wasn't hurt himself,' Polly thought, as she hung up her own receiver. 'It sounded like an awfully loud explosion.'

She saw the wolf a day or two later in the street. His face and head were covered with bandages, from amongst which one eye looked sadly out.

'Oh Wolf, I am so sorry,' said kind Polly, stopping as he was just going to pass her. 'Does it hurt very much? It must have been an awfully big explosion.'

'Explosion? Where?' said the wolf, looking eagerly up and down the street.

'Not here. At your home. When you rang me up the other day.'

'Oh that!' said the wolf airily. 'That wasn't really an explosion. Just a spark or two and a sort of bang, that's all. I just got the candle in the way of the wires and they melted together, or something. Nothing to get alarmed about, thank you, Polly.'

'But your face,' Polly said, 'the bandages. Didn't you get hurt in that explosion?'

'No. But that gum! Whee-e-e-w! I'll tell you what, Polly,' the wolf said impressively. 'Don't ever try and stick a beard or whiskers on top of where your fur grows, with spirit gum. It goes on all right, but getting it off is – well! If it had been my own hair it wouldn't have been more painful getting it off. Next time I'm going to have one of those beards on sort of spectacle things you just hook over your ears. Don't you think that would be better?'

'Much better.'

'Not so painful to take off?'

'I should think not,' Polly agreed.

'Well you just wait till I've got these bandages off,' the wolf said gaily, 'and then you'll see! My own mother wouldn't know me.'

Perhaps it took longer than Polly expected to grow wolf fur again: at any rate it was a month or two before Polly heard from the wolf again, and she had nearly forgotten his promise, or threat, of coming to find her. It was just before Christmas, and Polly was out with her mother doing Christmas shopping. The streets were crowded and the shop windows were gay with silver balls and frosted snow. Everything sparkled and shone and glowed, and Polly held on to Mother's hand and danced along the pavements.

'Polly,' said her mother. 'Would you like to go to the toy department of Jarold's? I've got to get one or two small things there, and you could look round. I think they've got some displays of model railways and puppets, and they generally have a sort of Christmas fair with Father Christmas to talk to.'

Polly said yes, she would very much, and they turned in at the doors of the enormous shop and took a luxuriant gilded lift up to the third floor, to the toy department. It really was fascinating. While her mother was buying coloured glass balls for the Christmas tree, and a snowstorm for Lucy, Polly wandered about and looked at everything. She saw trains and dolls and bears; she saw bicycles, tricycles, swings and slides, boats and boomerangs and cars and carriages. At last she saw an archway, above which was written 'Christmas Tree Land'. Polly walked in.

There was a sort of scene arranged in the shop itself, and it was very pretty. There were lots of Christmas trees, all covered with sparkling white snow, and the rest of the place was rather dark so that all the light seemed to come from the trees. In the distance you could see reindeer grazing, or running, and high snowy mountains and forests of more Christmas trees. At the end of the part where Polly was, sat Father Christmas on a sort of throne. There was a crowd of children round him and a man in ordinary clothes, a shop manager, was encouraging their mothers to bring them up to Father Christmas so that they could tell him what they hoped to find in their stockings or under the tree on Christmas Day.

Polly drew near. She thought she would tell Father Christmas that what she wanted more than anything else in the world was a clown's suit. She joined a line of children waiting to get up to the throne.

The child in front of Polly was frightened. She kept on running out of line back to her mother, and her mother kept on putting her back in her place again.

'I don't want to go and talk to that Father Christmas,' the little girl said, 'he isn't a proper Father Christmas.'

'Nonsense,' her mother said sharply. 'Don't be so silly. Stand in that line and go up and tell him what you want in your stocking like a nice little girl.'

The little girl began to cry. Polly, looking sharply at Father Christmas, couldn't help rather agreeing with her. Father Christmas had the usual red coat and hood and a lot of bushy white hair all over his face. But somehow his manner wasn't quite right.

He certainly asked the children questions, but not in the pleasantest tone of voice, and his reply to some of their answers was more of a snarl than a promise.

The little girl in front of Polly was finally persuaded to go up and say something in a breathy, awestruck whisper. Polly, just behind her, was near enough to hear the answer.

'Box of sweets,' said Father Christmas in a distinctly unpleasant tone. 'What do you want a box of sweets for? You're quite fat enough already to satisfy any ordinary person, I should think.'

The child clutched her mother's hand tightly, and the manager who was standing near, looked displeased. 'Come, come,' Polly heard him say sharply in Father Christmas's ear, 'you can do better that that, surely.'

Father Christmas jumped, threw a sharp glance over his shoulder at the manager and leant forward to the little girl. 'Yes, of course you shall have a box of sweets,' he said. 'Only wouldn't you like something more interesting? For instance a big juicy steak, with plenty of fried potatoes? Or what about pork chops? I always think myself there's nothing like ...'

'Next please,' the manager called out loudly. 'And a happy Christmas to you, dear,' he added to the surprised little girl who was being led away by her mother, unable to make head or tail of this extraordinary Father Christmas.

Polly moved up. The Father Christmas inclined his ear towards her to hear what she wanted in her stocking, but Polly had something else to say.

'Wolf, how could you!' she hissed in a horrified whisper. 'Pretending to be Father Christmas to all these poor little children – and you're not doing it at all well, either.'

'It wasn't my fault,' the wolf said, gloomily. 'I never meant to let myself in for this terrible affair. I just put on my costume – and I did the beard rather well this time, don't you think? – and I went out to see if I could find you, and this wretched man' – and he threw a glance of black hate at the shop manager – 'nobbled me in the street, and pulled me in here, and set me to asking the same stupid question of all these beastly children. And they all want the same things,' he added venomously. 'If it's boys they want space guns, and if it's girls they want party frocks and television sets. Not one of them's asked for anything sensible to eat. One of them did ask for a baby sister,' he said thoughtfully, 'but did she really want her to eat, I ask myself?'

'I should hope not,' Polly said firmly.

'And I'm much too hot and my whiskers tickle my ears horribly,' the wolf complained. 'And there's not a chance of snatching a bite with this man standing over me all the time.'

'Wolf, you wouldn't eat the children!' Polly said in protest.

'Not all of them,' the wolf answered. 'Some of them aren't very –'

'Next please,' said the manager loudly. A deliciously plump juicy little boy was pushed to stand just behind Polly. He was reciting to himself and his mother, 'I want a gun, an' I want soldiers, an' I want a rocking 'orse, an' I want a steam engine, an' I want . . .'

'I think you're going to be busy today,' Polly said, 'I probably shan't be seeing you for a time. Happy Christmas,' she added politely, as she made way for the juicy little boy. 'I hope you enjoy yourself with all these friendly little girls and boys.'

'Grrrrrr,' replied Father Christmas. 'I'll enjoy myself still more when I've unhooked my beard and got my teeth into one unfriendly little girl. Just you wait, Polly: Christmas or no Christmas, I'll get you yet.'

CATHERINE STORR

A Fishy Tale

Or How I Joined the Mixed Maggots and Bottom Feeders, Told to Gene Kemp by John Sweet

My Dad says the best thing to do is to forget all about it. Especially as I lost my wellingtons. I suppose he's right, really, but since you asked about it, here goes, Mzz Kemp.

I was getting tired, I reckon, and my concentration slipped and so did I, into the canal, at the edge where all the tall plants and reeds line the bank, deep and green and mysterious, full of insects and weird crawlies. And there in the middle of the canal is the deep channel where all the fish swim along. Yes, I love fishing. I like going fishing with my Dad better than anything else. Better even than football, I think ... All them fish, browny red dace, roach with orange fins, spotted perch, all spiky, you need a rag to protect your hands when you get him off the hook, and down at the bottom of the centre channel there's the spotted brown gudgeon, a bottom feeder, and the stone loach with stick-out lips, like this, whuwh, see? Of course you do get the nobs putting in a grand appearance sometimes, the salmon and the silver brown trout, but not for me with my licence at £1.50. If you do nabble one, you put it back quick.

Oh, it's a fantastic sport.

And the sport isn't just to catch the fish, but to land it, easy, easy. If you wind in too quickly the line will break, because of the friction, so you must do it slowly to let it move around in angles which tires the fish, and it's easier to pull out smoothly. Don't let the line go loose or the fish jumps, the hook slides and the fish escapes.

You need the feel, like.

This Sunday I'm telling you about, my Dad took me out about four. It was a smashing day, hot for October, with brown and yellow leaves lying in heaps to shuffle your feet through, scrunch, scrunch. I was glad to go, not only because, as I've told you, I like going fishing with my Dad better than anything, but because it had been that sort of a Sunday. My elder brother was out of the house somewhere, but the rest were hanging about all over the place, shouting and bossing me about, that's the worst of having four sisters, and you know what our Sandra is like, Mzz Kemp. Our house isn't very big neither, and my Mum made me do jobs, but it didn't really matter, not inside, because I knew I was going fishing with my Dad.

We set off, and it was still warm and sunny, though the mist was beginning to stir in little smoky spirals as we walked down the long hill that goes to the river and beyond to the canal. It's called Fore Street, and our teacher, you, Mzz Kemp, told us the Romans marched down there, long ago, and people before that, and it's a pretty steep hill, though that didn't bother me, *then*.

At last we reached the canal, and there's a road on one side for cars, and a path on the other for people and dogs, but half-way to Double Locks is a bridge, a really narrow bridge, and there the road crosses over, becoming a path, and the path becomes the road on the other side, bit daft really, not that it bothered me and Dad, because we were walking anyway, but it is tricky to drive across. Two posts stop cars trying to drive on to the path. Just beyond the bridge, where it's fine for fishing with the banks all green and quiet and beautiful, I sat down with my tackle and Dad wandered on a bit. I put down my bag for the fish and my rag to handle them with, then I made sure the eyes were level, pulled the lines up through them, fixed the little round band, the float and the hook, judged the weights, put them on, stood up straight and cast without maggots. Then I got the maggots on to the hook, pushing them with my thumb, and cast. My landing net was ready and the float was okay. The red bit goes under when you've got a bite.

Only I hadn't. And I didn't. I waited and I waited and I waited.

The sun painted the sky, pink and purple and orange and red, while I sat there on my little folding stool, waiting. No bite at all.

Not a sausage. Not a dicky bird. Not a dicky bird of a sausage. Not a nibble.

I could feel a nibble inside, though.

I was hungry. I was very hungry. I was starving.

Roast pork with apple sauce and crackling when we got home, Mum had said. I thought about roast pork and apple sauce and crackling. I pictured it on my plate. I pictured me eating it. I felt even hungrier.

The sun pushed off to the other side of the world or wherever it goes, taking all the colour with it. Grey mist trailed everywhere. My fingers grew cold and stiff. Dad came along and asked how I was doing, no good I said, him neither, we'd pack it in soon and go home.

'Another minute, Dad,' I asked, as he turned away. I didn't want to return with no catch and Sandra laughing like a drain, and I don't know why, but at the very thought of Sandra, my chair slipped, so did I, and there I was, slip, sliding away on my back into the reeds, and down, down, down into the water, coming up over my wellies, colder than cold, shock, horror. Somehow I turned, grabbed a rough and unkind sort of plant and yelled for Dad, who had gone some way away.

And a car came over the bridge, a man's head stuck out of the window, yelling. 'Look at that little kid. He's gonna drown! Stop!'

It didn't stop. It came roaring on. Towards me. My cold hands were slipping. Any minute now, I'd be among the fish I'd been after, earlier, and I didn't fancy the idea much. I didn't want to meet the bottom feeders on their own level. I didn't think we'd have much to say to each other down there amongst all that cold mud. 'Dad!' I yelled even louder. I couldn't see him, and I was slipping further all the time.

But if I couldn't see Dad, I could see the car. It was heading straight towards me and it didn't look as if it knew how to stop. It seemed as if I had a choice. Either be run over or drowned. I thought fast, very fast. And there was only one way to go so I went. Backwards into the canal. Right up to my neck in cold slimy canal right down into what seemed enough mud to submerge a submarine. I thought I could hear the fishes laughing all the way to Double Locks.

The car swerved, hitting the posts, one went into the water, just missing me, the other stayed put and the car rose up on it. The back door flew open and out jumped a man.

'Don't worry, son. I'm here.'

He certainly was. Water splashed everywhere, as if some huge whale was spouting off. He grabbed me by the neck and headed for the bank.

'I'm all right. I can swim,' I shouted, but he wasn't listening. Holding me like he was a dog with his favourite bone, he stumbled on, then fell forward, me with him.

'I can't swim,' he shouted, dropping me, and waving his arms about.

'I'm coming,' shouted another man, leaping towards us. I managed to move just in time. This splash was more like a freak tidal wave. Nowhere was left untouched. But I'd seen Dad on the bank and I was getting to him fast.

'It's all right,' shouted my Dad. 'Don't all go in!'

Too late. Another flying body hit the water, now full of bodies and one post. The canal was having a busy evening. Together we arrived at the bank where Dad pulled us out one by one. A lot of panting and spitting and coughing went on. That canal water doesn't taste nice at all.

'We saved your boy,' said one.

'Yeah,' said my Dad.

'Aren't you gonna thank us?'

'Well, thank you, yes, and I hope you enjoyed your bit of fun in there, but I feel I must say that first of all. he's the school swimming champion, and next, you couldn't drown a rabbit in there, let alone three big blokes like you. John, where's your wellingtons?'

'In the mud, Dad. They came off.'

'Well, we'd better get walking then, before you catch cold. It's a fair step.'

The driver had righted the car by now. The others climbed in dripping wet.

'We can't offer you a lift,' one said.

'Funny you not being able to swim, Reg. I never knew that,' I heard one of them say. Reg made a sort of angry roaring noise as the car drove off.

It was a long way home. Especially in wet-socked feet. And I thought I'd got a fish down my back, but it turned out to be a slimy weed. I kept thinking of them Roman soldiers as we walked back up that hill, Mzz Kemp, and how they had to keep going when they didn't feel like it. Once a dog came out and barked at us, but he soon stopped when my Dad said a few words to him. But it was a long way home.

Roast pork and apple sauce and crackling's scrumptious when you eat it in front of a hot fire after a bath. Even Sandra was nice to me. She didn't laugh. Much.

Guess what I'm doing next Sunday?
Going fishing, of course.

GENE KEMP

THE BORING BEAR

One day Julie came to John's house. She hung her coat on the low peg in the hall, then she saw something unusual.

'Why's this bear hiding under the coats?' she said.

'Because he's boring,' said John.

'He looks all right,' said Julie.

'That's all he does,' said John. 'He always looks like that.'

Julie looked at the bear. His face wasn't sad or happy. It was printed on, like his clothes: black trousers and red jacket, printed buttons, printed pockets.

'My gran made him,' said John. 'He's got washable stuffing.'

Then he put the bear back under the coats and they played monsters. They often played monsters. They liked being a little bit frightened.

When Julie put her coat on to go home, she looked at the bear. He was quite smart.

'Can I have him?' she said.

John thought.

'I'll swop him for your bell,' he said.

Julie's tricycle was old, but the bell was new. She'd rung it a lot for the first week, but she did like the look of the bear.

'All right,' she said.

So bear and bell changed hands.

When John went to Julie's house, he hung his anorak on the low peg in the hall. He saw a paw he'd seen before. 'Why's my bear hiding under the coats?' he said.

'He's Bear now,' said Julie. 'He likes it there. He thinks it's a warm, dark cave. He jumps out and frightens people.'

John brought Bear into the light. He was the same underneath, black trousers and all, but he looked different on top. He was wearing a blue sweater with the sleeves rolled back, he had a patch over one eye and a bandaged leg.

'What did he do?' said John.

'He fell off a mountain,' said Julie. 'I pushed him.'

John looked more closely.

'It's a good bandage,' he said. 'What can he do today?'

'Well, if his leg's better, the bandage can come off,' said Julie.

'And the leg?' said John.

'No,' said Julie. 'He'll need both legs for exploring. He's Action Bear. We can make him an exploring kit.'

John made Bear a paper hat for hot weather and wound string round his shoulder for a climbing rope. Julie drew a map in case he got lost.

Then her mother gave them some iron rations. Iron rations are not nails and things, you know; more dates and cheese and chocolate, if you're lucky.

At last they set off. They hauled themselves upstairs, then they pulled Bear up by his climbing rope. Then suddenly they heard noises.

'Monsters,' said Julie and they rushed downstairs while Bear slid down the bannister.

'He's hurt his arm,' said John. 'I'll make a sling.'

Then they sat on the bottom stair and ate their iron rations.

'Can I have him back now?' said John.

'No,' said Julie.

That week John rode his tricycle a lot. He rang the bell until his thumb was tired and so was everyone else.

'It's time that fire engine went home,' said his mother.

The next time Julie came to John's house, she was carrying a big shopping bag, and looking out was Bear. He still had a patch over one eye, but this time he was wearing a wooden sword in his string belt.

'He's very fierce,' said Julie, 'but he knows me.'

'And me,' said John. 'My gran's coming this week.'

Julie thought. Her tricycle was a bit quiet without the bell.

'All right,' she said. 'You can have him back. Do you want the sword?'

'No,' said John. 'I'll make one.'

He liked making things for Bear.

The next day John's gran really did come. Bear was lying near the fire after a hard day. His leg was bandaged, his arm in a sling.

'Goodness,' she said. 'Is that the bear I made?'

'Yes,' said John. 'With washable stuffing.'

'I thought he might be too dressed up,' said his gran. 'A bit boring.'

'His clothes don't take off,' said John, 'they put on. You never know what he'll do next.'

'I can see he isn't boring now,' said his gran.
Perhaps, thought John, he never was.

JOAN WYATT

The Seventh Princess

Did you ever hear the tale of the Six Princesses who lived for the sake of their hair alone? This is it.

There was once a King who married a gypsy, and was as careful of her as if she had been made of glass. In case she ran away he put her in a palace in a park with a railing all round it, and never let her go outside. The Queen was too loving to tell him how much she longed to go beyond the railing, but she sat for hours on the palace roof, looking towards the meadows to the east, the river to the south, the hills to the west, and the markets to the north.

In time the Queen bore the King twin daughters as bright as the sunrise, and on the day they were christened the King, in his joy, asked what she would have for a gift. The Queen looked from her roof to the east, saw May on the meadows, and said:

'Give me the Spring!'

The King called fifty thousand gardeners, and bade each one bring in a root of wild-flowers or a tender birch-tree from outside, and plant it within the railing. When it was done he walked with the Queen in the flowery park, and showed her everything, saying:

'Dear wife, the Spring is yours.'

But the Queen only sighed.

The following year two more Princesses, as fair as the morning, were born, and once again, on their christening day, the King told the Queen to choose a gift. This time she looked from the roof to the south, and, seeing the water shining in the valley, said:

'Give me the river!'

The King summoned fifty thousand workmen and told them to conduct the river into the park that it should supply a most beautiful fountain in the Queen's pleasure grounds.

Then he led his wife to the spot where the fountain rose and fell in a marble basin, and said:

'You now have the river.'

But the Queen only gazed at the captive water rising and falling in its basin, and hung her head.

Next year two more Princesses, as golden as the day, were born, and the Queen, given her choice of a gift, looked north from the roof at the busy town, and said:

'Give me the people!'

So the King sent fifty thousand trumpeters down to the market-

place, and before long they returned, bringing six honest market-women with them.

'Here, dear Queen, are the people,' said the King.

The Queen secretly wiped her eyes, and then gave her six beautiful babies into the charge of the six buxom women, so that the Princesses had a nurse apiece.

Now in the fourth year the Queen bore only one daughter, a little one, and dark like herself, whereas the King was big and fair.

'What gift will you choose?' said the King, as they stood on the roof on the day of the christening.

The Queen turned her eyes to the west, and saw a wood-pigeon and six swans flying over the hills.

'Oh!' cried she, 'give me the birds!'

The King instantly sent fifty thousand fowlers forth to snare the birds. While they were absent the Queen said:

'Dear King, my children are in their cots and I am on my throne, but presently the cots will be empty and I shall sit on my throne no more. When that day comes, which of our seven daughters will be Queen in my stead?'

Before the King could answer the fowlers returned with the birds. The King looked from the humble pigeon, with its little round head sunk in soft breast-feathers, to the royal swans with their long white necks, and said:

'The Princess with the longest hair shall be Queen.'

Then the Queen sent for the six nurses and told them what the King had said. 'So remember,' she added, 'to wash and brush and comb my daughters' hair without neglect, for on you will depend the future Queen.'

'And who will wash and brush and comb the hair of the Seventh Princess?' they asked.

'I will do that myself,' said the Queen.

Each nurse was exceedingly anxious that her own Princess should be Queen, and every fine day they took the children out into the flowery meadow and washed their hair in the water of the fountain, and spread it in the sun to dry. Then they brushed it and combed it till it shone like yellow silk, and plaited it with ribbons, and decked it with flowers. You never saw such lovely hair as the Princesses had, or so much trouble as the nurses took with it. And wherever the six fair girls went, the six swans went with them.

But the Seventh Princess, the little dark one, never had her hair washed in the fountain. It was kept covered with a red

handkerchief, and tended in secret by the Queen as they sat together on the roof and played with the pigeon.

At last the Queen knew that her time had come. So she sent for her daughters, blessed them one by one, and bade the King carry her up to the roof. There she looked from the meadows to the river, from the markets to the hills, and closed her eyes.

Now, hardly had the King done drying his own, when a trumpet sounded at his gate, and a page came running in to say that the Prince of the World had come. So the King threw open his doors, and the Prince of the World came in, followed by his servant. The Prince was all in a cloth of gold, and his mantle was so long that when he stood before the King it spread the whole length of the room, and the plume in his cap was so tall that the tip touched the ceiling. In front of the Prince walked his servant, a young man all in rags.

The King said:

'Welcome, Prince of the World!' and held out his hand.

The Prince of the World did not answer; he stood there with his mouth shut and his eyes cast down. But his Ragged Servant said, 'Thank you, King of the Country!' And he took the King's hand and shook it heartily.

This surprised the King greatly.

'Cannot the Prince speak for himself?' he asked.

'If he can,' said the Ragged Servant, 'nobody has ever heard him do so. As you know, it takes all sorts to make the world: those who speak and those who are silent, those who are rich and those who are poor, those who think and those who do, those who look up and those who look down. Now, my master has chosen me for his servant, because between us we make up the world of which he is Prince. For he is rich and I am poor, and he thinks things and I do them, and he looks down and I look up, and he is silent, so I do the talking.'

'Why has he come?' asked the King.

'To marry your daughter,' said the Ragged Servant, 'for it takes all sorts to make a world, and there must be a woman as well as a man.'

'No doubt,' said the King. 'But I have seven daughters. He cannot marry them all.'

'He will marry the one that is to be Queen,' said the Ragged Servant.

'Let my daughters be sent for,' said the King, 'for the time is now come to measure the length of their hair.'

So the Seven Princesses were summoned before the King. The six fair ones came in with their nurses, and the little dark one came in by herself. The Ragged Servant looked quickly from one to another, but the Prince of the World kept his eyes down and did not look at any of them.

Then the King sent for the court tailor, with his tape-measure; and when he came the six fair Princesses shook down their hair till it trailed on the ground behind them.

One by one they had it measured, while the six nurses looked on with pride – for had they not taken just as much care as they could of their darlings' hair? But, alas! as neither more care nor less had been spent upon any of them, it was now discovered that each of the six Princesses had hair exactly as long as the others.

The Court held up its hands in amazement, the nurses wrung theirs in despair, the King rubbed his crown, the Prince of the World kept his eyes on the ground, and the Ragged Servant looked at the Seventh Princess.

'What shall we do,' said the King, 'if my youngest daughter's hair is the same length as the rest?'

'I don't think it is, sir,' said the Seventh Princess, and her sisters looked anxious as she untied the red handkerchief from her head. And indeed her hair was not the same length as theirs, for it was cropped close to her head, like a boy's.

'Who cut your hair, child?' asked the King.

'My mother, if you please, sir,' said the Seventh Princess. 'Every day as we sat on the roof she snipped it with her scissors.'

'Well, well!' cried the King, 'whichever is meant to be Queen, it isn't you!'

That is the story of the Six Princesses who lived for the sake of their hair alone. They spent the rest of their lives having it washed, brushed, and combed by the nurses, till their locks were as white as their six pet swans.

And the Prince of the World spent the rest of *his* life waiting with his eyes cast down until one of the Princesses should grow the longest hair, and become his Queen. As this never happened, for all I know he is waiting still.

But the Seventh Princess tied on her red handkerchief again, and ran out of the palace to the hills and the river and the meadows and the markets; and the pigeon and the Ragged Servant went with her.

'But,' she said, 'what will the Prince of the World do without you in the palace?'

'He will have to do as best he can,' said the Ragged Servant, 'for it takes all sorts to make the world, those that are in and those that are out.'

ELEANOR FARJEON

MR ANTONIO

Mr Antonio was small and dark with a nice wiggly moustache, and he didn't just sell ice cream – he *made* it. It was soft and creamy and he had learned how to make it from his mother.

Mr Antonio and his mother came from a country called Italy, where they make a lot of ice cream. It's the place where the very first ice cream was made.

Mr Antonio made strawberry ice cream, vanilla ice cream, chocolate ice cream and pistachio – that's the one with the nuts inside.

Mr Antonio put his ice cream into little plastic boxes, and then he put the plastic boxes inside a big plastic box.

After that he put the big plastic box inside a big wooden box on the front of his tricycle. Then, he would ride along the road, ringing his bell . . .

Every day Mr Antonio would cycle along a straight road with tall trees on each side, up a hill, down the other side, and over a little bridge to the village where the children lived.

When he arrived Mr Antonio rang his bell and all the children came running out of their houses to buy an ice cream.

'You tell me what you want,' said Mr Antonio, 'I gotta strawberry ice cream, vanilla ice cream, chocolate ice cream and pistachio – that's the one with the nuts inside.'

One morning, it was raining, but Mr Antonio made his ice cream, put it into little plastic boxes and those little plastic boxes were put inside a big plastic box. After that the big plastic box was put inside the big wooden box on the front of Mr Antonio's tricycle.

Mr Antonio cycled along the straight road with tall trees on each side, up the hill and then ... oh dear, the road was wet and going down the hill he went faster, and faster. The tricycle started to slide and slide, and then fell over, and it rolled over and over until it stopped at the bottom of the hill.

Poor Mr Antonio got up, brushed the mud off his trousers and put his tricycle back on its wheels. He rang his bell ... and it still worked, but when he looked inside the ice cream box, the lids had fallen off the little plastic boxes and all the ice cream was mixed up.

Poor Mr Antonio felt very unhappy, and pushed his tricycle along the road, over the bridge and into the village. He didn't ring his bell, but the children still came running out to buy their ice cream.

'Hello,' said Mr Antonio, 'I'm sorry but my tricycle fell over and all the ice cream is mixed up together,' and he lifted the lid of the ice-cream box to show them.

'That's all right,' said one little boy, 'I like things all mixed up. It's like the trifle my mum makes, I'll call it *trifle* ice cream.'

Now, when Mr Antonio rings his bell and the children come running out, he says: 'I gotta strawberry ice-a-creama, vanilla ice-a-creama, chocolate ice-a-creama, pistachio – that's the one with the nuts, and I got *trifle* ice-a-creama.'

He makes it specially, all the flavours mixed up together, because the children like it so much.

DAVID WILLMOTT

The Dutch Doll

Once upon a time there was a little girl called Jenny.

One day her uncle gave her a shining fivepenny piece and she carried it about with her, tied in the corner of her handkerchief.

'Will you buy some sweets?' asked her father.

'Will you buy a book?' asked her mother.

'No,' said Jenny and shook her head. She knew what she was going to buy. She was going to buy a Dutch doll.

In the town where Jenny lived there was a market every Saturday. The market people came and set up tables and stalls right in the middle of the main street and on these they put all kinds of things to sell – fish and flowers and eggs and cabbages and clothes and books and toys.

Jenny loved going to the market, and there was one stall she liked better than all the others. It belonged to an old lady. Every Saturday she sat there and sold Dutch dolls, all costing exactly five pence each.

When Saturday came, Jenny asked her mother to take her to the market, so that she could choose her Dutch doll. Mother held her hand and they made their way through the crowds till they came to the old lady with her Dutch dolls.

The Dutch dolls had wooden heads and wooden bodies and wooden arms and wooden legs. Their arms were jointed at the elbow so that they could move up and down. The legs were jointed at the knee, so that they could move too.

Each doll had black shining hair painted on her flat wooden head, and black eyes and red lips, and a dab of red on each cheek as well. And a sharp little wooden nose sticking out in the middle of her face.

Jenny looked at them all and wondered which she should choose. 'Hurry up and choose, Jenny,' said Mother. 'They are all just the same.'

Oh dear, Jenny did not know which doll she liked best! One had specially red cheeks. Another had specially black hair. Then she noticed one that had a sad look on her face. Jenny stared at her for a long time. She looked as if she were lonely. 'I'll have *this* one please,' said Jenny, and she picked up the sad-faced doll. She untied the knot in the corner of her handkerchief and took out the money and gave it to the old lady.

'I shall call my Dutch doll Greta,' said Jenny as they hurried away. Now on the way home they had to cross a bridge over the river. Jenny stopped, because she liked to look down at the boats and the swans in the water below. 'Look, Greta,' she said, and held the little Dutch doll up so that she could see too. 'Look at the boats and the two big swans. Aren't they nice?'

But Greta still looked sad.

Suddenly, someone who was walking by bumped into Jenny and Greta fell out of her hand, over the railing of the bridge, down, down, down till she hit the water – splash!

'Oh!' cried Jenny. 'Oh! She's gone! Greta's fallen in the water!'

Then Jenny heard another splash. A big black dog jumped into the water from the side of the river and swam towards Greta. He thought Jenny had thrown a stick in for him, and he liked getting sticks out of the water. Because Greta was made of wood, she floated on the top of the water. Soon the dog reached her and took her in his mouth and swam back to the side of the river where his master was waiting for him.

He jumped out and shook himself, 'Brr brr,' and then he laid Greta at his master's feet. He wagged his tail proudly and his master patted his wet head and said, 'Good dog! Good dog!'

'Wuff, wuff,' said the big black dog, for he wanted his master to throw Greta in again.

But his master said, 'No – good dog – lie down,' then they waited for Jenny and her mother to come.

Jenny hurried over the bridge and ran fast along the side of the river. When she got to the man she bent down and patted the big dog's wet head and said: 'Thank you for saving Greta; she's only new today.'

'I'm afraid my dog's teeth have made some marks on your new doll and scratched off some of her paint, but if you'll let me keep her till tomorrow I'll make her as good as new. Where do you live?'

'Ivy Cottage, just along the road there,' said Jenny, and she pointed so that he'd know the way.

'Leave her with me today,' said the man, 'and I'll bring her back on my way past your house tomorrow.'

'Thank you,' said Jenny, though she knew she'd miss Greta badly, and would rather have taken her home even if she was scratched a bit.

That afternoon Jenny made a nice bed all ready for Greta out of a shoe-box, and she made some toy food for her – red apples and white eggs and yellow buns.

And next morning, sure enough, the front-door bell rang, and there was the man with the big black dog. He handed Jenny a brown paper parcel and said, 'There she is, young lady, as good as new.'

'Thank you,' said Jenny. 'Would your dog like a bone for his dinner? We kept one for him.'

'Yes,' said the man. 'He would.'

So Jenny gave him a big, juicy bone, wrapped up in paper, and he went away.

And then Jenny undid her parcel and took out Greta and had a good look at her.

'Oh, Greta,' she said. 'Your hair is blacker than it was, and your cheeks are redder, *and you've got a smile*. You don't look sad any more. Did you like falling in the river then? Did it cheer you up?'

But Greta just went on smiling and looking happy, so Jenny put her to sleep in the nice new bed she had made for her.

RUTH AINSWORTH

JAMIE'S DISAPPEARING LUNCH

One day Jamie's mother packed his lunch in a box. She put in a cold sausage, two honey sandwiches, a red apple and some milk in a drink bottle. Jamie put his lunch into a bag with a long strap, and slung it over his shoulder like the postman. He climbed over his back fence and went into the paddock. Then Jamie sat down under a shady tree.

He opened his lunch box and took out the cold sausage. Just as he was going to take a bite, he saw a little white dog coming towards him. The dog's nose was sniffing along the ground and his tail was stuck up in the air. It was Scamp. He belonged to Jamie's friend, Mr Potter.

When Scamp saw the cold sausage in Jamie's hand he sat down. He put up his front paws to beg, as if to say, 'Mmmm, I'm hungry, Jamie!'

Jamie broke off a piece of his cold sausage. He threw it to Scamp who quickly gobbled it up. Jamie kept on throwing pieces of cold sausage to Scamp until it was all gone, and there was none left for Jamie.

Next, Jamie took out his sandwiches. Just as he was about to eat one, he saw lots of brown sparrows hopping around his feet. They cocked their little heads as if to say, 'We're hungry, Jamie!'

Jamie broke off little pieces of his sandwich and threw them to the sparrows. He kept on throwing pieces of his honey sandwiches until they were all gone, and there was none left for Jamie.

Then Jamie decided to have a drink of milk. He pulled the cork from his milk bottle. He was just going to drink some when he heard, '*Miaow, miaow!*' Jamie looked up. There was his own black cat, Fluff, running towards him. She must have followed Jamie from his house.

'*Miaow! miaow!*' wailed Fluff as if to say, 'I'm thirsty, Jamie!'

Jamie poured some of the milk into his lunch box and watched Fluff lap it up. Then he poured some more, and then some more, until it was all gone, and there was none left for Jamie.

He only had his red apple left. Just as he was about to bite into it, he heard *'Maaa! Maaa!'* Without looking round Jamie knew who was calling. It was Gerda, the little white goat who lived in the paddock where Jamie was having his picnic lunch.

Gerda was tied behind the tree where Jamie was sitting. He knew that she liked apples. He gave her his red apple and watched her munch it to the very last bit.

Now there was nothing left for Jamie to eat. He packed his lunch things into the bag and slung it over his shoulder like the postman, and he went home.

He said to his mother, 'I'm hungry, Mother!' And his mother packed him another lunch.

This time Jamie sat in his garden, and ate it all by himself.

RUTH JONES

THE QUEEN IS COMING TO TEA

Pixie Parks and her mum and dad were an ordinary family, who lived in an ordinary house in an ordinary street, next door to ordinary Mr and Mrs Jones.

One day the Queen said: 'I should like to visit an ordinary house to see how my ordinary subjects live.' So her secretary sent a letter to Mr and Mrs Parks, saying that the Queen would come to tea with them on Friday, the twenty-fifth of June.

The letter was long and gold, with a royal seal on it. Mrs Parks was all of a flutter when she read it.

She took out the best tablecloth and held it up. 'That's not good enough for the Queen!' she said. 'We must buy a new one.' And she went out shopping.

But the new tablecloth had a fancy fringe that tickled Pixie's knees.

'I liked the old tablecloth best,' said Pixie. 'Besides, this new one is too fancy for our plain white cups and saucers.'

'You are right!' Mrs Parks declared. 'We must buy a new tea-set!' And she went out shopping.

But the new cups had curly little handles. Mr Parks could not hold them properly in his big fingers. 'I liked the old cups best,' he said. 'Besides, this new tea-set is too fancy for our plain old table.'

'You are right!' Mrs Parks declared. 'We must buy a new table.' And she went out shopping.

But the new table was so well polished that Pixie's plate went sliding all over the place. 'I liked the old table best,' said Pixie. 'Besides, this new one is too shiny for our dull old chairs.'

'You are right!' Mrs Parks declared. 'We must buy new chairs!' And she went out shopping.

But the new chairs had hard seats, and no little spindles to rest your feet on.

'We liked the old chairs best,' said Pixie and her dad. 'Besides, these new chairs are too fancy for our faded old carpet.'

'You are right!' Mrs Parks declared. 'We must buy a new carpet!' And she went out shopping.

But when the new carpet was laid, Mr Parks had to take off his boots every time he came into the room. 'I liked the old carpet best,' said Mr Parks. 'Besides, this new one is too fancy for our old dresser.'

'You are right!' Mrs Parks declared. 'We must buy a new dresser!' And she went out shopping.

But the new dresser had no room for books, or the pictures Pixie painted, or Mr Parks's pipes. 'We liked the old dresser best,' said Pixie and her dad. 'Besides, all this fine furniture is too grand for our little dining-room.'

'You are right!' Mrs Parks declared. 'We must move house at once!'

So Mr and Mrs Parks moved to a splendid new house. It had a fine, big garden with a fountain, a goldfish pond and statues made

of marble. It had sixteen windows, and a glass part at the side where plants were growing. But that house was far too big for the three of them. Pixie got lost upstairs, and Mr Parks got lost in the garden. 'We liked the old house best,' said Pixie and her dad.

Besides, the new house was not an ordinary house, so the

Queen did not want to see it. She went to tea with Mr and Mrs Jones instead.

HAZEL TOWNSON

WHAT WE NEED IS A NEW BUS

Not so long ago an old red bus ran down to the station and back again. It was a rumbling-grumbling bus. It was a rusty-dusty bus. It was a jumping-bumping bus. And because it was all of these things some people walked to the station rather than ride in the old bus. It shook them about too much.

'The trouble with this old bus,' the driver said, 'is that it's worn out. It needs a new engine to drive it. It needs new tyres to run on. It needs new seats, new windows, new paint, new everything. In fact what we need is a *new* bus!'

Now the bus wasn't surprised to hear this. It did feel worn out. It was worn out. Climbing the hills made its engine work so hard it went slower and slower and slower. Changing gears all the time made it feel exhausted. All it wanted to do was sleep in the sun for ever.

'*Ur, ur, ur!*' it grumbled. It didn't want to go another wheel turn.

Inside the bus the conductor was calling out, 'Fares, pliz! Fares! Fares, pliz!' He sold pink tickets from his book to the passengers, and their money dropped into his big black bag with a tinkling plink, plink, plink.

And inside the bus the driver was in his seat in front of the big steering wheel. He pushed the gear lever into place. He pulled off the brake and before it knew what was happening the old red bus was rolling down the road again.

'*Urr-uuuuur*-urrrr-urrrrr!' It grumbled. It mumbled. It groaned. '*Grrrr!*' It was as if it couldn't go another wheel turn. And to its surprise the old red bus didn't.

Sssssss!

The front tyre was shrinking smaller and smaller. *Sssssssss!* What was happening to the plump round sides? *Sssssssss!* Air hissed out. The tyre was as flat as a piece of paper.

The driver stopped the bus. Out he jumped. Out jumped the bus conductor. People poked their heads from their windows.

'The front tyre is as flat as a pancake,' the driver told them. 'We can't fix it here. You'd better walk to the station.'

'We'd better get the mechanic from the garage,' said the conductor. 'We could be here for hours,' he told the people. 'Yes, you'd be better off walking to the station.'

Now the people grumbled and mumbled and groaned and moaned and walked to the station. 'What we need is a new bus,' they muttered and some of them stopped to look at the flat tyre that had run over a big nail. It had stabbed a hole in the tyre's tube. *Sssssss!* Out hissed the air until the tyre, no longer fat and round, looked saggy-baggy, as flat as flat. A sad limp tyre.

When, at last, the mechanic came roaring up in his truck he tapped the old red bus with a spanner and said, 'This old crate needs more than a new tyre.'

'I know, I know,' agreed the bus driver. 'What we need is a new bus. When can you sell us one?'

'Not today.' The mechanic shook his head. He banged and tapped and looked at the insides of the bus and said nothing for a long time, then he said, 'In a couple of weeks we could make this old bus almost as good as new, up at the garage.'

Now that was a good idea. A wonderful idea, especially for the old bus. It helped as much as it could when the tow-truck came. There was a crane on the back of the tow-truck and it lifted the front wheels of the bus away, away off the ground. With just its two back wheels the old red bus ran along behind the tow-truck to the garage.

And when some people saw the old red bus being towed away they decided that it must be going to the scrap-heap. Where else could it go? 'Looks as if we'll get a new bus after all,' they told each other.

At the garage, mechanics took out the worn parts of the engine and put in new ones. They oiled and greased. They fitted new tyres and new seats. They repainted and repainted the old bus a sparkling red, a shiny red, a geranium red. It didn't look like an old bus. It didn't feel like an old bus. It felt like running a thousand miles or two – up hills, down hills and along lumpy, bumpy roads.

When the time came for the old red bus to drive along the road to the station everyone wanted a ride. They crowded in. Some people sat and some people had to stand. The bus was loaded but up the hill it went without a grumble or rumble, just a little *gr-grr-grrr* which was like a happy humming song. 'This isn't bad for our old red bus!' said the conductor with a grin.

'Not our old rumbling, grumbling bus!' shrieked someone. 'This can't be our old, dusty, rusty bus! Don't tell me that this is the bumpy, jumpy, worn-out old bus!'

It was, and we know that it was, don't we?

JEAN CHAPMAN

THE SECRET OF THE STAIRS

Jo fell down the cellar stairs. As she rolled, she landed on each step.

Thunk

Thunk

Thunk

Thock

Thunk

'That was odd,' she thought.

Falling downstairs was not odd.

Jo was nearly two years old and was always falling downstairs.

It was one of the steps which was odd.

It had made a strange noise when she landed on it.

Jo went back upstairs for her ball and gently pushed it over the edge of the first step. She listened to the sound of the ball as it slowly bounced down the stairs.

Boing

Boing

Boing

Bonk

Boing

Boing

There it was again. What could it mean?

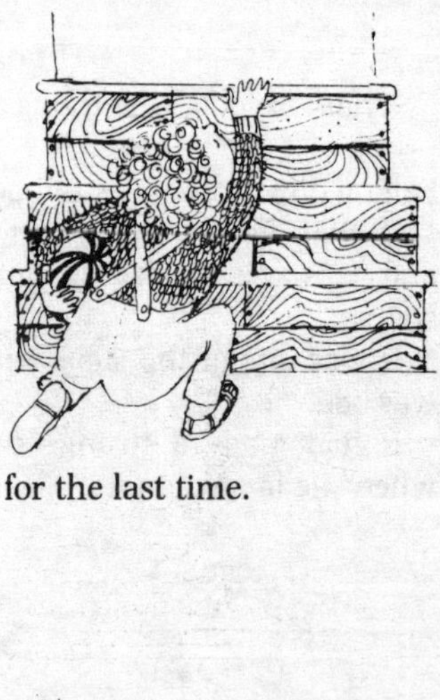

Jo bumped down the steps on her bottom. She picked up her ball from the cellar floor and clambered back upstairs.

She heard her mother shout at her again to stop playing on the stairs. She had been shouting at them ever since they had arrived at their new house.

Their father said she worried too much.

Jo pushed the ball down the steps for the last time.

Boing

Boing

Boing

Bonk

Boing

Boing

This time her sister, Catherine, noticed it too.

Catherine left the dusty trunk of old plates she had discovered in a corner, and came to see.

She stamped noisily up the stairs to Jo.

They both listened to the sound of her feet.

Dunt

Dunt

Dunt

Donk

Dunt

Dunt

It was the third step from the bottom which was odd.

They both sat on the fourth step and stared down between their feet.

The steps were wooden. The third one from the bottom had two cracks in it.

Jo drummed her feet, just for fun.

The cracks moved a little. There was a loose plank.

Catherine found her last lolly stick in her pocket. She pushed it into one of the cracks and prised up the plank. They turned it over. Underneath, it was covered in soft, grey, woolly cobwebs thick with dust.

Jo stroked it.

Catherine rolled some into little balls to put on the plates she had found.

Later, peering into the dark hole they had made under the stairs, they saw a piece of cloth. Catherine lifted it out. It was a little bag. She pulled it open, breaking the faded ribbon around it.

Jo put the ribbon on her head. They both laughed.

Catherine emptied the bag on to Jo's lap.

There, on her knee, gleamed a heap of gold coins.

They looked like chocolate Christmas-tree money but they were hard and heavy. They clinked when Jo dropped them through her fingers.

'I know,' whispered Catherine, 'let's keep them in the bag, under the stairs, and we won't tell anyone and we can pretend it's our real treasure.'

And that is just what they did.

LYNNE RUSSELL

WHAT HAPPENED TO MUSTARD

This is a story about Mustard, the little yellow cat, and about something that happened to him not very long ago.

One morning he was sitting on the grass in the front garden. He had been very busy washing himself, licking his paw and wiping it round and round his face. Now he was quite clean. He didn't know what to do next, so he just sat and watched the road beyond the front garden, waiting for something to happen.

Very soon something did happen. A great big van, the biggest van Mustard had ever seen, stopped outside the garden gate. It was a green van, with yellow letters painted on it, and it was even bigger than the coalman's lorry, and *that* was the biggest thing Mustard knew. Presently two men, wearing white aprons, got down from the driving seat at the front and walked round to the back of the van. Mustard couldn't quite see what they were doing but ... clank ... clank ... clank ... clank ... what a noise! The men pulled down the back of the van, for it was really a sort of door.

Mustard ran across the grass and climbed quickly up one of the trees by the gate so that he could see right into the van. It was almost empty. Only a few sacks and boxes were inside. The two men in white aprons opened the garden gate and walked up to the front door of the house.

'I wonder what they want?' thought Mustard. 'I've never seen them before.'

He sat on the branch of the tree and his green eyes watched and watched. They watched the men go back to the van and bring the sacks and boxes indoors. Mustard could hear the men's heavy boots clumping about the house. 'Clump ... clump ... clump ... clump!' they went. It sounded as if they were walking on floors which had no carpets on them.

'Goodness me!' said Mustard to himself. 'Look what they are doing now! They are taking away the blue carpet from the hall and putting it into the big van. What *can* be happening?'

He watched the men bring out some more rolls of carpet. Then they brought out some chairs, then a table, then a sideboard, then a cupboard, and then ... and *then* ... they brought out Mustard's basket, Mustard's very own round basket with the brown cushion in it. And they put the basket into the van, with the carpets and the chairs and the table and the sideboard and the cupboard.

'Well!' said Mustard. 'My basket! Well!'

As soon as the men had gone inside the house again, Mustard jumped down from the tree and ran out of the front gate. He saw a wooden board which stretched like a hill from the ground to the floor of the big van. Up the hill he ran and into the van he pranced. This was fun.

'Miaow, miaow!' he laughed, showing his little pink tongue. 'Miaouw, miaouw.'

He ran round and round the inside of the big van, jumping on the chairs and on the table. And then, behind the cupboard, he found ... his very own basket. He jumped into the basket and curled himself round on the soft brown cushion.

'A ... a ... a ... ah! Mia-a-o-w!' he sighed. 'I *am* so tired.'

It was quite dark in that corner of the van behind the cupboard, and in a few minutes Mustard was fast asleep. He stayed asleep for a long time, and then suddenly, 'Clank ... clank ... clank ... clank!' What a noise! Mustard opened his eyes. Where *was* he?

What was this strange, dark place full of tables and chairs and cupboards and rolls of carpet? Oh, yes! Of course! He was inside the big van. And the clank ... clank ... clank ... clank must have been the noise the men made when they shut the van doors.

'Oh dear!' cried Mustard, sitting up in his basket. 'Oh miaow, miaow! I'm shut in.'

Now he could hear the children calling him from the front garden.

'Mustard!' they called. 'Mustard, where are you?'

'Miaow, miaow!' cried the little yellow cat.

'Mustard! Come along! We're going in the car to the new house and we want to take you with us.'

'Miaow! Here I am! Miaow!' called Mustard, from the inside of the van.

But the children couldn't hear him. They were terribly worried, for they couldn't think where he could be.

'Honk! Honk!' went the horn on the van. 'Honk! Honk!' And the big, green van began to move slowly away, with the yellow cat shut up inside it.

Mustard lay down again in his basket behind the cupboard. He didn't know where they were going, nor what was happening. But it was very comfortable on his nice brown cushion, and he was having a lovely ride.

After a little while, the van began to slow down. Then it stopped altogether.

'Clank ... clank ... clank ... clank!' What a noise! The men were opening the door at the back of the van. Mustard jumped out of his basket and ran towards them.

'Why, here's a little cat!' said one man.

'Oh, Mustard! Darling Mustard! He must have been in the moving van all the time. And we thought he was lost.'

'Miaow!' cried Mustard happily.

'Come and see the new house, Mustard. Come along! This is where we're all going to live now.'

They picked him up and carried him into the house.

'We'll bring the little cat's basket indoors in a minute,' promised one of the white-aproned men.

The children said, 'Thank you very much,' and then they hugged Mustard more tightly than ever.

'What a clever little cat!' they said. 'He found the new house all by himself.'

'Miaow!' said Mustard. And because he loved being hugged and stroked he purred as loudly as he could. Brr ... brr ... brr ... brr ...

DORIS RUST

THE MICE AND THE CHRISTMAS TREE

Now you shall hear the story about a family of mice who lived behind the larder wall.

Every Christmas Eve, Mother Mouse and the children swept and dusted their whole house with their tails, and for a Christmas tree Father Mouse decorated an old boot with spider's web instead of tinsel. For Christmas presents, the children were each given a little nut, and Mother Mouse held up a piece of bacon fat for them all to sniff.

After that, they danced round and round the boot, and sang and played games till they were tired out. Then Father Mouse would say, 'That's all for tonight! Time to go to bed!'

That is how it had been every Christmas and that is how it was to be this year. The little mice held each other by the tail and danced round the boot, while Granny Mouse enjoyed the fun from her rocking-chair, which wasn't a rocking-chair at all, but a small turnip.

But when Father Mouse said, 'That's all for tonight! Time to go to bed!' all the children dropped each other's tails and shouted: 'No! No!'

'What's that?' said Father Mouse. 'When I say it's time for bed, it's time for bed!'

'We don't want to go!' cried the children, and hid behind Granny's turnip rocking-chair.

'What's all this nonsense?' said Mother Mouse. 'Christmas is over now, so off you go, the lot of you!'

'No, no!' wailed the children, and climbed on to Granny's knee. She hugged them all lovingly.

'Why don't you want to go to bed, my little sugar lumps?'

'Because we want to go upstairs to the big drawing-room and dance round a proper Christmas tree,' said the eldest Mouse child. 'You see, I've been peeping through a crack in the wall and I saw a huge Christmas tree with lots and lots of lights on it.'

'We want to see the Christmas tree and all the lights too!' shouted the other children.

'Oh, but the drawing-room can be a very dangerous place for mice,' said Granny.

'Not when all the people have gone to bed,' objected the eldest Mouse child.

'Oh, do let's go!' they all pleaded.

Mother and Father Mouse didn't know what to say, but they couldn't very well disappoint the children on Christmas Eve.

'Perhaps we could take them up there just for a minute or two,' suggested Mother Mouse.

'Very well,' said Father, 'but follow me closely.'

So they set off. They tiptoed past three tins of herring, two large jars of honey, and a barrel of cider.

'We have to go very carefully here,' whispered Father Mouse, 'not to knock over any bottles. Are you all right, Granny?'

'Of course I'm all right,' said Granny. 'You just carry on. I haven't been up in the drawing-room since I was a little Mouse girl; it'll be fun to see it all again.'

'Mind the trap!' said the eldest Mouse child. 'It's behind that sack of potatoes.'

'I know that,' said Granny. 'It's been there since I was a child. I'm not afraid of that!' And she took a flying leap right over the trap and scuttled after the others up the wall.

'What a lovely tree!' cried all the children when they peeped out of the hole by the drawing-room fireplace. 'But where are the lights? You said there'd be lots and lots of lights, didn't you? Didn't you?' the children shouted, crowding round the eldest one, who was quite sure there had been lights the day before.

They stood looking for a little while. Then suddenly a whole lot of coloured lights lit up the tree! Do you know what had happened? By accident, Granny had touched the electric switch by the fireplace.

'Oh, how lovely!' they all exclaimed, and Father and Mother and Granny thought it was very nice too. They walked right round the tree, looking at the decorations, the little paper baskets, the glass balls, and the glittering tinsel garlands. But the children found something even more exciting: a mechanical lorry!

Of course, they couldn't wind it up themselves, but its young master had wound it up before he went to bed, to be ready for him to play with in the morning. So when the Mouse children clambered into it, it started off right away.

'Children, children! You mustn't make such a noise!' warned Mother Mouse.

But the children didn't listen; they were having a wonderful time going round and round and round in the lorry.

'As long as the cat doesn't come!' said Father Mouse anxiously.

He had hardly spoken before the cat walked silently through the open door.

Father, Mother and Granny Mouse all made a dash for the hole in the skirting but the children were trapped in the lorry, which just went on going round and round and round. They had never been so scared in all their Mouse lives.

The cat crouched under the tree, and every time the lorry passed she tried to tap it with her front paw. But it was going too fast and she missed.

Then the lorry started slowing down. 'I think we'd better make a jump for it and try to get up the tree,' said the eldest Mouse. So when the lorry stopped they all gave a big jump and landed on the branches of the tree.

One hid in a paper basket, another behind a bulb (which nearly burned him), a third swung on a glass ball, and the fourth rolled himself up in some cotton wool. But where was the eldest Mouse? Oh yes, he had climbed right to the top and was balancing next to the star and shouting at the cat:

Silly, silly cat
You can't catch us!
You're much too fat,
Silly, silly cat!

But the cat pretended not to hear or see the little mice. She sharpened her claws on the lorry.

'I'm not interested in catching mice tonight,' she said as if to herself. 'I've been waiting for a chance to play with this lorry all day.'

'Pooh! That's just a story!' said the eldest who was also the bravest. 'You'd catch us quick enough if we came down.'

'No, I wouldn't. Not on Christmas Eve!' said the cat. And she kept to her word. When they did all come timidly down, she never moved, but just said: 'Hurry back to your hole, children. Christmas Eve is the one night when I'm kind to little mice. But woe betide you if I catch you tomorrow morning!'

The little mice pelted through that hole and never stopped running till they got to their home behind the larder wall. There

were Father and Mother and Granny Mouse waiting in fear and trembling to know what had happened to them.

When Mother Mouse had heard their story she said, 'You must promise me, children, never to go up to the drawing-room again.'

'We promise! We promise!' they all shouted together. Then she made them say after her The Mouse Law, which they'd all been taught when they were tiny:

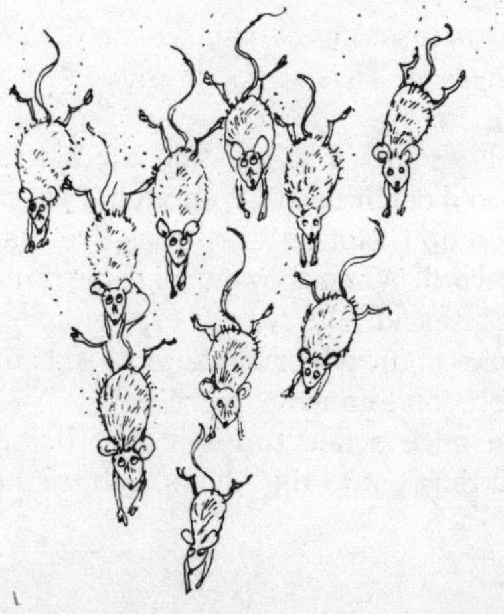

We promise always to obey
Our parents dear in every way,
To wipe our feet upon the mat
And, never, never cheek the cat.

Remember too the awful danger
Of taking money from a stranger;
We will not go off on our own
Or give our mother cause to moan.

Odd bits of cheese and bacon-scraps
Are almost certain to be traps,
So we must look for bigger things
Like loaves and cakes and doughnut-rings;

And if these rules we still obey
We'll live to run another day.

ALF PRØYSEN

INDEX OF TITLES

Index of Authors

ACKNOWLEDGEMENTS

The editor and publishers gratefully acknowledge permission to reproduce copyright material in this book:

'Eggs' by Joan Aiken, reprinted by permission of the author; 'The Dutch Doll' by Ruth Ainsworth, reprinted by permission of the Estate of Ruth Ainsworth; 'Miss Hickory' from *Miss Hickory* by Carolyn Sherwin Bailey, copyright © 1946 by Carolyn Sherwin Bailey, copyright renewed © by Rebecca Davies Ruan, 1974. Reprinted by permission of Hodder and Stoughton Ltd and by permission of Viking Penguin Inc.; 'The Paper Palace' from *The Elephant Party and Other Stories* by Paul Biegel (Kestrel Books), reprinted by permission of Penguin Books Ltd; 'The Pudding Like a Night on the Sea' from *The Julian Stories* by Ann Cameron, reprinted by permission of Victor Gollancz Ltd; 'What We Need is a New Bus' by Jean Chapman, reprinted by permission of the author; 'The Seventh Princess' from *The Little Bookroom* by Eleanor Farjeon, reprinted by permission of Les Editions Denoël Gonthier Planete and Blackie and Son Ltd; 'A Bunch of Flowers' by René Goscinny, reprinted by permission of Les Editions Denoël Gonthier Planete and Blackie and Son Ltd; 'The Farm Brothers' Band' by Ursual Hourihane from *The Second Read-to-Me Story Book*, reprinted by permission of Methuen Children's Books; 'The Dragon Who Cheated' from *The Dribblesome Teapots* by Norman Hunter, reprinted by permission of the Bodley Head; 'A Fishy Tale' by Gene Kemp, reprinted by permission of the author; 'The Kidnapping of Clarissa Montgomery' copyright © Robin Klein, 1984, reprinted by permission of Curtis Brown Ltd, London; 'The Snowtime Express' copyright © 1962 by Lilian Moore, reprinted by permission of Marion Reiner for Lilian Moore; 'In the Middle of the Night' from *What the Neighbours Did and Other Stories* by Philippa Pearce (Kestrel permission of Penguin Books Ltd; 'The Mice and the Christmas Tree' from *Little Old Mrs Pepperpot* by Alf Prøysen reprinted by permission of Century Hutchinson Ltd; 'Jack Jackdaw' by Anne Rooke, reprinted by permission of the author; 'The Secret of the stairs' by Lynne Russell, reprinted by permission of the author; 'What Happened to Mustard' from *A Story a Day* by Doris Rust, reprinted by permission of Faber & Faber Ltd; 'Galldora and the Mermaid' from *New Adventures of Galldora* by Modwena Sedgwick, reprinted by permission of Harrap Ltd; 'Father Christmas' from *Adventures of Polly and the Wolf* by Catherine Storr, reprinted by permission of Faber & Faber Ltd; 'The Queen is Coming to Tea' by Hazel Townson, reprinted by permission of the author; 'Mr Antonio' by David Willmot, reprinted by permission of the author; 'The Boring Bear' by Joan Wyatt, reprinted by permission of the author.

Every effort has been made to trace copyright holders, but in a few cases this has proved impossible. The editor and publishers apologize for these unwilling cases of copyright transgression and would like to hear from any copyright holders not acknowledged.